*f*P

## ALSO BY STEPHEN R. COVEY

*The 8th Habit: From Effectiveness to Greatness*
*The 7 Habits of Highly Effective People*
*The 7 Habits of Highly Effective People Workbook*
*The 7 Habits of Highly Effective People Journal*
*The 7 Habits of Highly Effective Families*
*Living the 7 Habits*
*The Nature of Leadership*
*First Things First*
*Principle-Centered Leadership*

## ALSO FROM FRANKLINCOVEY CO.

*The 6 Most Important Decisions You'll Ever Make: A Guide for Teens*
*The 7 Habits of Highly Effective Teens*
*The 7 Habits of Highly Effective Teens Workbook*
*The 7 Habits of Highly Effective Teens Journal*

*Life Matters*
*businessThink*
*What Matters Most*
*The 10 Natural Laws of Successful Time and Life Management*
*The Power Principle*
*Breakthrough Factor*

# THE 8th HABIT®

*Personal Workbook*

STEPHEN R. COVEY

FREE PRESS
*New York London Toronto Sydney*

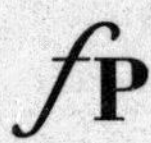

FREE PRESS
A Division of Simon & Schuster, Inc.
1230 Avenue of the Americas
New York, NY 10020



First Free Press trade paperback edition 2006



For information regarding special discounts for bulk purchases,
please contact Simon & Schuster Special Sales:
1-800-456-6798 or business@simonandschuster.com

Manufactured in the United States of America

10 9 8 7 6 5 4 3 2 1

ISBN-13: 978-0-7432-9319-8
ISBN-10: 0-7432-9319-3

# CONTENTS

# About This Personal Workbook

The world has changed profoundly since *The 7 Habits of Highly Effective People* was published in 1989. The challenges and complexity we face in our personal lives and relationships, in our families, in our professional lives, and in our organizations are of a different order of magnitude. So, are the 7 Habits still relevant in today's new reality? Absolutely—the greater the change and more difficult the challenges, the *more* relevant they become. Being highly effective as individuals and organizations is no longer optional in today's world—it's the price of entry to the playing field.

*The 8th Habit* represents the pathway to the enormously promising side of today's reality. Its purpose is to give you a road map that will lead you from pain and frustration to true fulfillment, relevance, significance, and contribution in today's new landscape, not only in your work and organization, but in your whole life. In fact, it is a timeless reality. It is the voice of the human spirit—full of hope and intelligence, resilient by nature, boundless in its potential to serve the human good. The 8th Habit is: Find Your Voice and Inspire Others to Find Theirs. This voice encompasses the soul of organizations that will survive, thrive, and profoundly effect the future of the world.

The promise of *The 8th Habit* is that, if you will be patient and take the time to understand the root problem, then set a course of living the timeless, universal principles embodied in the solution outlined in the book, your influence will steadily grow from the inside out. You will find your voice and will inspire your team and organization to find theirs in a dramatically changed world.

This companion personal workbook to *The 8th Habit* is designed to help you take the quantum leap from effectiveness to greatness. It's a hands-on, mind-on, heart-on process. The first part of each workbook chapter will help you deepen your understanding by reviewing the underlying principles found in the book and completing brief exercises. At the end of each chapter you will find application exercises to help you begin living the principles. I encourage you to mark up and flag particularly meaningful pages or exercises to which you may want to return later.

Making this quantum leap from effectiveness to greatness takes time. The following Schedule Suggestions section outlines various ways to approach the material.

## SCHEDULE SUGGESTIONS

You have at least four options to apply what you learn using *The 8th Habit* and this companion personal workbook:

1. The first approach is to simply read the book straight through, then decide what you want to apply to your life and work and complete those areas in this personal workbook.
2. The second approach is to read the book straight through, then go back and read it a second time as you complete this personal workbook.
3. The third approach, one I personally believe is most beneficial, is to adopt a year-long personal development program. The table below outlines how to read *The 8th Habit* and complete the personal workbook over the course of twelve months. You'll notice this approach referred to throughout the personal workbook. Should you choose a different approach, simply ignore the references to the month-long focus for each chapter.
4. The fourth approach is to simply adapt the timeline below to fit your needs.

| Time | Focus Area |
|---|---|
| Preparation | • Read Chapters 1–3 and complete the corresponding chapters in this workbook to deepen your understanding and lay the groundwork for your year-long focus. |
| Month 1 | • Read Chapter 4 and Appendix 1 and complete the corresponding chapter in this workbook.<br>• For the remainder of the month, select and complete activities from "Applying Your Knowledge." |
| Month 2 | • Read Chapter 5 and complete the corresponding chapter in this workbook.<br>• For the remainder of the month, select and complete activities from "Applying Your Knowledge." |
| Month 3 | • Read Chapter 6 and complete the corresponding chapter in this workbook.<br>• For the remainder of the month, select and complete activities from "Applying Your Knowledge." |
| Month 4 | • Read Chapter 7 and complete the corresponding chapter in this workbook.<br>• For the remainder of the month, select and complete activities from "Applying Your Knowledge." |
| Month 5 | • Read Chapter 8 and complete the corresponding chapter in this workbook.<br>• For the remainder of the month, select and complete activities from "Applying Your Knowledge." |
| Month 6 | • Read Chapter 9 and complete the corresponding chapter in this workbook.<br>• For the remainder of the month, select and complete activities from "Applying Your Knowledge." |

| Time | Focus Area |
|---|---|
| Month 7 | • Read Chapter 10 and complete the corresponding chapter in this workbook.<br>• For the remainder of the month, select and complete activities from "Applying Your Knowledge." |
| Month 8 | • Read Chapter 11 and complete the corresponding chapter in this workbook.<br>• For the remainder of the month, select and complete activities from "Applying Your Knowledge." |
| Month 9 | • Read Chapter 12 and complete the corresponding chapter in this workbook.<br>• For the remainder of the month, select and complete activities from "Applying Your Knowledge." |
| Month 10 | • Read Chapter 13 and complete the corresponding chapter in this workbook.<br>• For the remainder of the month, select and complete activities from "Applying Your Knowledge." |
| Month 11 | • Read Chapter 14 and complete the corresponding chapter in this workbook.<br>• For the remainder of the month, select and complete activities from "Applying Your Knowledge." |
| Month 12 | • Read Chapter 15 and complete the corresponding chapter in this workbook.<br>• For the remainder of the month, select and complete activities from "Applying Your Knowledge." |
| Reinforcement | • Review and complete the activities outlined in the "Renewal Activities Calendar" in the "Appendices." |

As you work through this personal workbook, you will complete application exercises, take notes, record your thoughts, score yourself on self-assessments and answer questions designed to provoke thought and encourage deeper insights into the reading material. You will also be asked to review film clips from the companion DVD included with *The 8th Habit* hardcover book or available for viewing online at *www.The8thHabit.com/offers* with *The 8th Habit* paperback book. Simply insert the DVD into your home DVD player or computer DVD drive and select the desired film, or go online and select the desired film. At the beginning of each section, you will be asked to read or reread specific chapters in *The 8th Habit*. *The 8th Habit* and this personal workbook are designed to be companions, so use them and reuse them!

To effectively complete this personal workbook, the chapter content needs to be fresh in your mind. You can do this in one of three ways: Read the chapter (or reread the chapter), then immediately complete the corresponding chapter in this workbook, read the section at the beginning of each chapter in this workbook titled "Reviewing the Underlying Principles" or read the chapter summaries located in the "Appendices" of this workbook.

## THE 8TH HABIT CHALLENGE

This personal workbook is also designed to help you complete the 8th Habit Challenge, if you desire. The chart at the back of *The 8th Habit* book will help you track your progress. Once you have completed the entire challenge chart, you may certify you have done so at *www.The8thHabit.com/challenge*, and receive a special recognition for your accomplishment.

I hope this workbook will empower you to learn and relearn your unique personal significance and that you will enjoy doing it. Give yourself the opportunity to really dig into the material presented in this workbook. Be honest with yourself and with others as you share your insights and the things you've learned. Make this material work for you!

*Chapter* 1

# THE PAIN

*Before you begin this section of the workbook, read pages 1–11 in* The 8th Habit, *review the underlying principles listed here or read the summary in the Appendix.*

> *All that is necessary for the triumph of evil is that good men do nothing.*
>
> —EDMUND BURKE

## REVIEWING THE UNDERLYING PRINCIPLES

- The birth of the Information/Knowledge Worker Age increased and changed the challenges and complexities we face in our personal lives and relationships. These challenges are of a different order of magnitude than in the past.
- FranklinCovey polled 23,000 workers and asked them various questions relating to their job satisfaction, their sense of contribution and their engagement and enthusiasm for their work. Only 37 percent said they have a clear understanding of what their organization is trying to achieve and why. Only one in five was enthusiastic about their team's or organization's goals. Only one in five workers said they have a clear "line of sight" between their tasks and their team's or organization's goals.
- Before the Information/Knowledge Worker Age, the call was for *effectiveness.* Now the call is for *greatness.*

- Tapping into the higher reaches of human genius and motivation requires a new mind-set—a new habit. The 8th Habit is a third dimension to the other 7 Habits; it is *Find Your Voice and Inspire Others to Find Theirs.*
- Voice is *unique personal significance.* Voice lies at the center of talent (your natural gifts and strengths), passion (those things that naturally excite and motivate you), need (including what the world needs enough to pay you for) and conscience (a voice within you that assures you of what is right and that prompts you to actually do it). When you engage in work that taps your talent and fuels your passion, therein lies your voice, your calling, your soul's code.
- Each of us has a deep, innate, almost inexpressible yearning to find our voice in life.
- The purpose of this book is to give you a road map that will lead you from this pain and frustration to true fulfillment, relevance, significance and contribution in today's new age.

## LEARNING OBJECTIVES

If you study and apply the underlying principles in this chapter, you can expect to:

- Gain an increased awareness of the challenges of the future and the mind-set required to succeed in that future.
- Begin the process of discovering your voice by thinking about your talents, passion and conscience, and how these areas can serve particular needs around you.
- Clarify how you can contribute in the areas of living, loving, learning and leaving a legacy.

**RELATING TO THE PAIN**

Look at the voices listed on page 1 in *The 8th Habit*. Do you relate to any of these voices? Which example(s) did you relate to the most?

___

___

___

Do you experience pain each day that is not expressed in any of the voices on page 1? What painful reality do you deal with? Describe it here.

___

___

___

___

___

Review the statistics on pages 2–3 in *The 8th Habit*. In what ways can you or your organization relate to these statistics?

___

___

___

**FINDING YOUR VOICE**

Look at the diagram. Let's begin to examine what your voice might be—your unique personal significance.

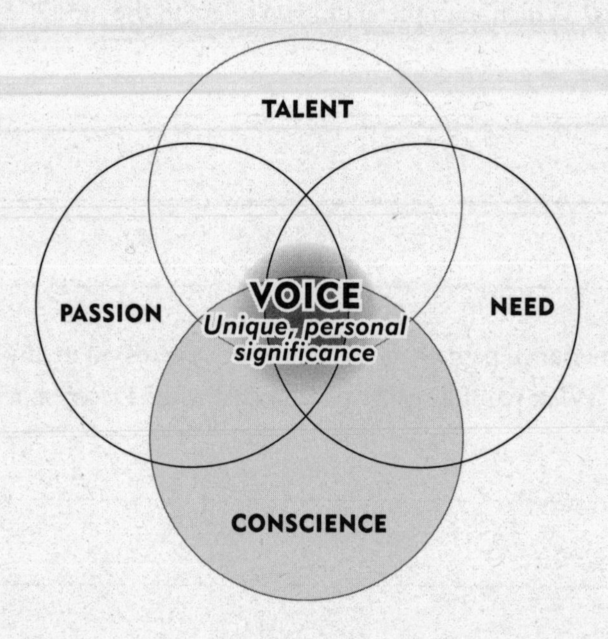


*Talent.* What do you feel are your natural gifts and strengths?

______________________________________________

______________________________________________

______________________________________________

______________________________________________

______________________________________________

______________________________________________

*Passion.* What things naturally energize, excite, motivate and inspire you?

How do your talents and passions connect to your organization's purpose?

*Need.* What skills do you have that you think the world needs enough to pay you for?

______________________________

______________________________

______________________________

______________________________

______________________________

______________________________

*Conscience.* Have you ever felt something within you that assured you of what was right, then prompted you to do it? Describe your experience.

______________________________

______________________________

______________________________

______________________________

______________________________

______________________________

______________________________

______________________________

In general, do you feel you have found your voice and vision in life? ______

If yes, *The 8th Habit* can help you clarify and deepen your purpose. If no, *The 8th Habit* can help you define and find your voice.

We'll talk in more detail about finding your voice in Chapters 4 and 5.

## VIEWING THE FILM *Legacy*

As you view the film *Legacy* on your companion DVD or online, list below how you would like to contribute in the following areas.

Living: ____________________________________________

____________________________________________

____________________________________________

____________________________________________

____________________________________________

____________________________________________

Loving: ____________________________________________

____________________________________________

____________________________________________

____________________________________________

____________________________________________

____________________________________________

Learning: ____________________________________________

____________________________________________

____________________________________________

____________________________________________

____________________________________________

____________________________________________

Leaving a Legacy: ____________________________________________

____________________________________________

____________________________________________

____________________________________________

____________________________________________

____________________________________________

## APPLYING YOUR KNOWLEDGE

Chapters 1–3 are introductory chapters to lay the groundwork for *The 8th Habit: Find Your Voice and Help Others to Find Theirs.* As such, the application sections in these three chapters are relatively short.

- Pick one principle you learned from this chapter and choose to make a change in your life. For example, based on the Muhammad Yunus story, you may decide to look more closely around you for people in need and to serve them.

Principle you learned: ______________________________

Action you will take: ______________________________

______________________________

______________________________

______________________________

______________________________

______________________________

______________________________

- Teach the main ideas of this chapter to at least two other people. List their names.

______________________________

______________________________

- Report your results to friends, colleagues and family members. List their names.

______________________________

______________________________

______________________________

______________________________

*Chapter* 2

# THE PROBLEM

*Before you begin this section of the workbook, read pages 12–24 in* The 8th Habit, *review the underlying principles listed here or read the summary in the Appendix.*

> *People decide how much of themselves they will give to their work depending on how they are treated and on their opportunities to use all four parts of their nature—*
> *physical, social/emotional, mental, and spiritual.*

### REVIEWING THE UNDERLYING PRINCIPLES

- Each age of history has transitioned to a new age that had exponential gains in productivity. Our ability to enter a new age and experience such increased results is dependent upon our willingness to change our view or paradigm.
- We are now in the Information/Knowledge Worker Age, yet organizations everywhere are operating and managing people with the mind-set of the Industrial Age. People are often treated as things needing to be managed and controlled. This type of treatment creates codependent relationships of disempowerment.
- If you want minor, incremental changes and improvements, work on practices, behavior, or attitude. But if you want to make significant, quantum-leap improvements, work on paradigms. The power of an accurate paradigm is that it first explains the world, then it guides behavior.

The Knowledge Worker Age is based on a new paradigm—the Whole-Person Paradigm.

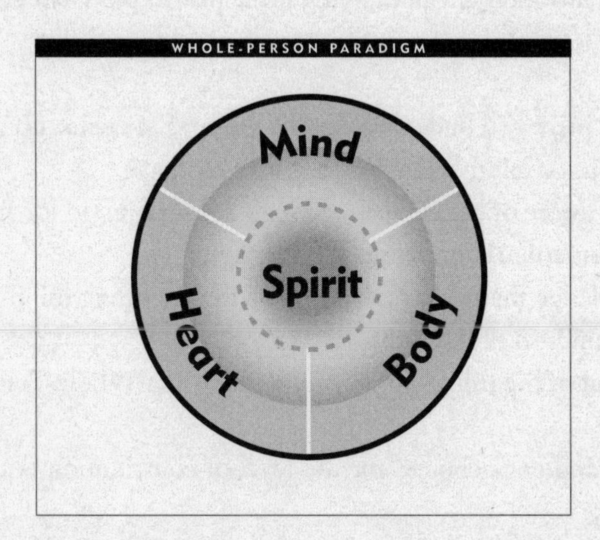


- The Whole-Person Paradigm reflects the four basic needs of every person: to live (body), to love (heart), to learn (mind) and to leave a legacy (spirit).
- Based on how we are treated and on our opportunities to use all four parts of our nature, we tend to make choices as outlined in the figure below.

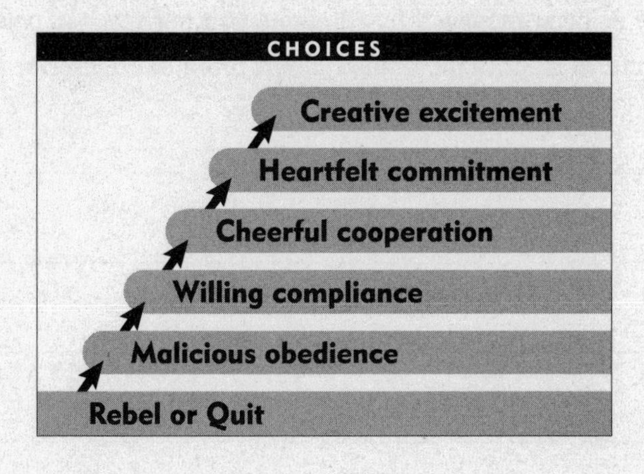

## LEARNING OBJECTIVES

If you study and apply the underlying principles in this chapter, you can expect to:

- Gain an increased understanding of the ages of civilization and the paradigms or mind-sets associated with each age.
- Become aware of the choices and paradigms required for success in the Information/Knowledge Worker Age.
- Acknowledge the part you have played in the thing mind-set, that is, the mind-set of the Industrial Age.
- Break out of the thing mind-set and move to a Whole-Person Paradigm.
- Understand your choices for the level of contribution you choose to make.
- Describe the results of your current paradigms and envision the new paradigms you will need to be successful in the Information/Knowledge Worker Age.

## UNDERSTANDING THE THING MIND-SET OF THE INDUSTRIAL AGE

Have you ever been managed by someone you felt was too controlling, authoritative and/or stuck in the Industrial Age mind-set? Describe the situation.

___

___

___

___

Did you respond well to being treated with the thing mind-set or the carrot-and-stick philosophy? How did you feel under this type of management?

Did you feel empowered to change your situation? Why or why not?

What could you have done to apply the insights you've gained in Chapter 2 to this situation?

Speculate how applying these insights would have changed your situation. Describe what may have happened.

Have you ever managed someone at work or at home using control tactics and the thing mind-set? Describe the situation.

_______________________________________________

_______________________________________________

_______________________________________________

_______________________________________________

_______________________________________________

_______________________________________________

_______________________________________________

Did others respond well to this type of management? How do you think the people you were managing felt?

_______________________________________________

_______________________________________________

_______________________________________________

_______________________________________________

_______________________________________________

_______________________________________________

_______________________________________________

How did you feel while managing using the thing mind-set?

What could you have done to apply the insights you've gained in Chapter 2 to this situation?

Speculate how applying these insights would have changed your situation. Describe what may have happened.

## VIEWING THE FILM *Max & Max*

After you view the film *Max & Max* on your companion DVD or online, answer the following questions.

What actions contributed to the final outcome of Max the employee and Max the dog?

________________________________________

________________________________________

________________________________________

________________________________________

________________________________________

________________________________________

________________________________________

________________________________________

If you were in a situation like this (either as Max or Mr. Harold), what could you do to change? How?

________________________________________

________________________________________

________________________________________

________________________________________

## LEARNING THE POWER OF A PARADIGM

The word *paradigm* means a perception, assumption, theory, frame of reference or lens through which you view the world.

Describe a paradigm that you think others have of you.

How does this paradigm affect how others treat and respond to you?

___

___

___

___

___

Are you happy with the results or outcomes of this paradigm? Why or why not?

___

___

___

___

___

What are some of your most deeply held paradigms of the world, other cultures, your organization, your department, your team, your family? List specific paradigms.

___

___

How do these paradigms influence your actions? List specific actions for each paradigm you wrote above.

Are you happy with the results or outcomes of these paradigms? Why or why not?

What paradigms will have to change for you to be a player in the Information/Knowledge Worker Age?

___

___

___

___

What will it take for your department, team or family to achieve greatness in the Information/Knowledge Worker Age?

___

___

___

___

## ACKNOWLEDGING THAT PEOPLE HAVE CHOICES

Think again about the Whole-Person Paradigm (see page 11)—the paradigm in which we acknowledge the body, mind, heart and spirit of each person. Ultimately, people choose how much of their talent, creativity and passion they will volunteer in their work. When any one of the four elements is missing from a situation, you will rarely break through to the cheerful cooperation, heartfelt commitment, or creative excitement levels that are possible for each situation outlined in the table. If you neglect any one of the four parts of human nature, you may begin to see people as things who need to be controlled, managed or carrot-and-sticked to be motivated. The best way to achieve breakthrough results is by breaking through to the higher levels where you are truly engaged and able to contribute to your greatest potential.

Place a check mark in the column that best describes your response to the situations described below.

| | Rebel or quit | Malicious obedience | Willing compliance | Cheerful cooperation | Heartfelt commitment | Creative excitement |
|---|---|---|---|---|---|---|
| 1. You have a new position in a new department. You are not treated fairly: There is nepotism at play, and they refuse to pay the salary agreed to at the interview. | | | | | | |
| 2. You ask your new boss to discuss concerns you have about the direction the team is going on a big new project, and he treats you unkindly and refuses. | | | | | | |
| 3. At a team meeting, you and your team are asked to rate the success of a recently completed project. You enjoyed working on the team, but have a lot of ideas on how to improve the process. You know from past experience that your manager does not want new ideas—he wants you to agree that the project went smoothly. | | | | | | |
| 4. For six months now, you have been filling out a weekly job status report. It doesn't take long to complete, but you notice that your manager never reads it. | | | | | | |
| 5. You are a member of a talented team and thoroughly enjoy your work, but lately you notice that your manager has been invoicing clients for work your team has not completed. | | | | | | |
| **Total check marks in this category:** | | | | | | |

Key: Question 1: Absence of commitment to body, Question 2: Absence of commitment to heart, Question 3: Absence of commitment to mind, Question 4: Absence of commitment to spirit, Question 5: Absence of commitment to spirit.

Which column has the *most* check marks? ______________________

Which columns scored *no* check marks? ______________________

Why do you think this is? ______________________

______________________

______________________

______________________

______________________

______________________

______________________

______________________

______________________

## APPLYING YOUR KNOWLEDGE

Complete the following activities to prepare for your focus on *The 8th Habit*:

- Observe the behaviors in your environment that reflect the Industrial Age. Observe behaviors in your environment that reflect the Information/Knowledge Worker Age. Record the results you observe from each type of behavior in the journal at the back of this workbook.

- Observe people in your environment. Who has a Max-type relationship with a superior? What is happening that supports that dysfunctional relationship? What are the results? Record your findings in the journal at the back of this workbook.

- Teach the main ideas of this chapter to at least two other people. List their names.

______________________________

______________________________

- Report your results to friends, colleagues and family members. List their names.

______________________________

______________________________

______________________________

______________________________

*Chapter* 3

# THE SOLUTION

*Before you begin this section of the workbook, read pages 25–35 in* The 8th Habit, *review the underlying principles listed here or read the summary in the Appendix.*

> *Those organizations that reach a critical mass of people and teams expressing their full voice will achieve next-level breakthrough in productivity, innovation, and leadership in the marketplace and society.*

### REVIEWING THE UNDERLYING PRINCIPLES

- Significant cultural or organizational changes generally begin with one or two people. Regardless of their positions, these people first changed themselves from the inside out. In short, they found their voices first, then inspired others to find theirs.
- *The 8th Habit: Find Your Voice and Help Others to Find Theirs* is the two-part solution to the pain and problem we currently face in the new Information/Knowledge Worker Age.
- Everyone chooses one of two roads in life: greatness or mediocrity. The choice is yours, and you are making that choice every day.
- To cultivate the habit of greatness, knowledge, attitude and skill must intersect. This workbook will help you increase your knowledge and skill, which, in turn, may enable you to shift your paradigm and attitude.

## LEARNING OBJECTIVES

If you study and apply the underlying principles in this chapter, you can expect to:

- Acknowledge and believe in your power to change yourself and your situation.
- Identify areas of your life where you have found your voice and areas in which you are still searching for your voice.
- Understand the two roads available for everyone—greatness or mediocrity.

## FINDING YOUR VOICE

Deep within each one of us is an inner longing to live a life of greatness and contribution—to really matter, to really make a difference, to have a voice. In what areas of your life do you feel you have found your voice?

___

___

___

___

___

___

___

___

In what areas of your life are you still searching for your voice?

Describe an area in which you would like to make a difference.

How will you know that you have made a difference? What will you know, feel or do?

_______________________________________________

_______________________________________________

_______________________________________________

_______________________________________________

_______________________________________________

_______________________________________________

_______________________________________________

Describe a situation in which you merely acted in a "custodial role in the traditions of the past" and took the road of mediocrity.

_______________________________________________

_______________________________________________

_______________________________________________

_______________________________________________

_______________________________________________

_______________________________________________

_______________________________________________

What do you wish you had done differently? What actions could you have taken to choose the road to greatness in that situation?

### VIEWING THE FILM *Discovery of Character*

As you view the film *Discovery of Character* on your companion DVD or online, list below some points in the film that are meaningful to you.

During what times of your life have you felt stressed, burned out and lethargic about your work, as depicted in the beginning of the film?

______________________________________________

______________________________________________

______________________________________________

______________________________________________

______________________________________________

______________________________________________

During what times of your life have you felt passionate about your work, completely committed and excited about what you were doing, as depicted in the latter part of the film?

______________________________________________

______________________________________________

______________________________________________

______________________________________________

______________________________________________

______________________________________________

We'll talk in more detail about finding your voice in the next chapters.

## APPLYING YOUR KNOWLEDGE

Complete the following activities to prepare for your focus on *The 8th Habit*:

- Go to a quiet spot—someplace where you can focus and feel peace. Think about the current contributions you are making to your family, work and community. Take mental notes of areas where you feel you could improve your contribution by finding your voice.

- Teach the main ideas of this chapter to at least two other people. List their names.

______________________________________________

______________________________________________

______________________________________________

- Report your results to friends, colleagues and family members. List their names.

______________________________________________

______________________________________________

______________________________________________

______________________________________________

______________________________________________

*Chapter* 4

# DISCOVER YOUR VOICE—UNOPENED BIRTH-GIFTS

*Before you begin this section of the workbook, read pages 39–63 and 331–351 in* The 8th Habit, *review the underlying principles listed here or read the summary in the workbook Appendix.*

> *Our deepest fear is not that we are inadequate.*
> *Our deepest fear is that we are powerful beyond measure.*
> —MARIANNE WILLIAMSON

## REVIEWING THE UNDERLYING PRINCIPLES

- Discovering your voice requires that you open and use three innate birth-gifts: your freedom to choose, natural laws and principles and your four intelligences or capacities.

| "HARDWIRED" BIRTH-GIFTS |
| --- |
| (Mostly unopened) |
| ■ **Freedom and Power to Choose** |
| ■ **Principles (Natural Laws)**<br>▪ Universal<br>▪ Timeless<br>▪ Self-Evident |
| ■ **The 4 Intelligences/Capacities**<br>IQ MENTAL — EQ EMOTIONAL/SOCIAL<br>PQ PHYSICAL/ECONOMIC — SQ SPIRITUAL |

- The freedom to choose is the first birth-gift. Between stimulus and response is a space. Within that space, regardless of how large or small it may be, each person has the ability to choose. Therefore, people are not products of nature (their genes) or of nurturing (their environment and surrounding). They are products of their choices.

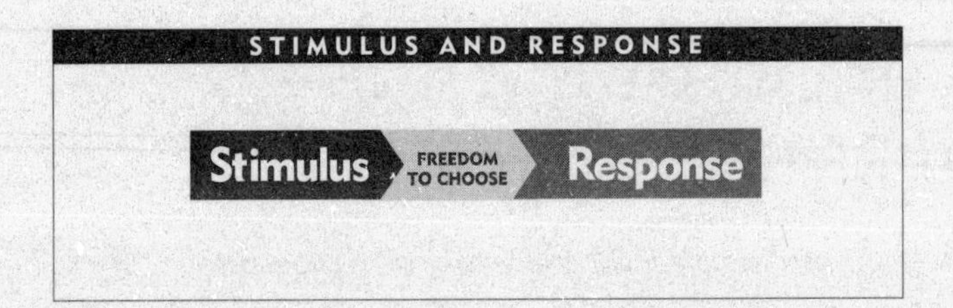


- Natural laws and principles are the second birth-gift.
  - *Natural laws and principles* are universal, timeless, objective and at work whether we agree with them or not.
  - *Natural authority* is the dominion of natural law.
  - *Moral authority* is the principled use of our freedom and power to choose. It requires the sacrifice of short-term selfish interests and the exercise of courage in subordinating social values to principles.
  - *Values* are social norms—they're personal, emotional, subjective and arguable.
  - Consequences are governed by natural laws and principles, and behavior is governed by values; therefore, value principles!

- The third birth-gift is the four intelligences or capacities of our nature, which can be categorized as mental intelligence (IQ), physical intelligence (PQ), emotional intelligence (EQ) and spiritual intelligence (SQ).

## LEARNING OBJECTIVES

If you study and apply the underlying principles in this chapter for a month, you can expect to:

- Increase your awareness and understanding of the birth-gifts that each person possesses.
- Use and increase your freedom-to-choose space between stimulus and response.
- Align your values with principles or natural laws to live with greater moral authority.
- Improve your mental, physical, emotional and spiritual intelligences or capabilities to help discover your voice.

## UNDERSTANDING THE FIRST BIRTH-GIFT: THE FREEDOM TO CHOOSE

Between stimulus and response is a space representing our freedom to choose. The key is to enlarge our freedom-to-choose space. What is the size of your reaction space? Circle the letter that best describes how you would react in these situations:

1. A co-worker comes into your cubicle at 5:00 P.M. with an urgent request for you to put together a pricing bid for a presentation he is making the next morning. He does not ask if you are in the middle of something or on your way out of the office. He simply expects you to stay late and help him with the numbers. How would you typically react?
   a. Calmly listen to his needs and suggest some alternatives to working late.
   b. Sympathize with your co-worker by saying, "Wow, that's a tough situation. I've been in that one before. I really feel for you. But unfortunately, I can't work late tonight." Then leave for the day.
   c. Instantly become offended and angry that he would expect overtime and extra work from you. Either agree to help or leave.

2. Your son asks to talk to you about extending his curfew hour. You've discussed his curfew three times already. You are tired of discussing it and wish he would just respect your wishes to be home by 10:00 P.M. on school nights. How would you typically react?

   a. Ask your son why he wants to talk about his curfew again, seeking to understand his needs and potentially changed circumstances.
   b. Tell your son that you don't want to spend hours rehashing the topic of curfew. Instead, tell him that he can stay out until midnight tonight only.
   c. Let out an exasperated sigh and tell him, "I am sick of talking about this! You come home when I tell you. Case closed!"

3. During your performance review with your boss, she tells you that several of your co-workers have complained that you are difficult to work with and aren't willing to put in extra effort. You are surprised because you haven't perceived a problem with your team. How would you typically react?

   a. You listen to what your boss has to say, then calmly ask for an example of the behavior to which she is referring. You brainstorm solutions to the perceived problem.
   b. You are hurt and stunned. You don't want your boss to think you are unprofessional, so you remain quiet throughout the remainder of the performance review. You silently vow to stay away from your co-workers and work independently for a while.
   c. You become defensive and demand, "Who said that? I want names and examples. I put in a lot more effort than half the people in this department. No one truly realizes my contribution!"

| | a | b | c |
|---|---|---|---|
| Total the amount of letters you circled: | | | |
| | Very large freedom-to-choose space | Medium freedom-to-choose space | Small freedom-to-choose space |

An awareness of your freedom and power to choose is affirming because it can excite your sense of possibility and potential. Read the following quote from R.D. Laing: "The range of what we think and do is limited by what we fail to notice. And because we fail to notice that we fail to notice, there is little we can do to change; until we notice how failing to notice shapes our thoughts and deeds."

How is becoming aware that you can choose (and are accountable for your choices) often frightening?

________________________________________

________________________________________

________________________________________

________________________________________

________________________________________

________________________________________

________________________________________

________________________________________

Anytime your emotional life is a function of someone else's weaknesses, you disempower yourself and empower those weaknesses to continue to interfere with your life. Describe a time when you were in a difficult situation, but let someone else's weakness create an emotionally stressful time for you.

______________________________________________

______________________________________________

______________________________________________

______________________________________________

______________________________________________

______________________________________________

How could creating a larger freedom-to-choose space have reduced the amount of time you spent in this situation?

______________________________________________

______________________________________________

______________________________________________

______________________________________________

______________________________________________

______________________________________________

## VIEWING THE FILM *Law of the Harvest*

After viewing the film *Law of the Harvest* on your companion DVD or online, answer the following questions.

What are the similarities between the law of the harvest (laws of nature) and human nature?

_______________________________________________

_______________________________________________

_______________________________________________

_______________________________________________

_______________________________________________

_______________________________________________

_______________________________________________

_______________________________________________

_______________________________________________

_______________________________________________

_______________________________________________

_______________________________________________

_______________________________________________

What is an example of how the law of the harvest starkly contrasts with our culture of quick fix, victimism and blame?

## UNDERSTANDING THE THIRD BIRTH-GIFT: THE FOUR INTELLIGENCES/CAPACITIES OF OUR NATURE

The four parts of our nature (body, mind, heart and spirit) correspond to four capacities, or intelligences. Developing and using these intelligences will instill within you quiet confidence, internal strength and security and personal moral authority. Your efforts to develop these intelligences will profoundly impact your ability to influence others and inspire them to find their voice.

The four intelligences (physical, mental, emotional and spiritual) are tightly interconnected. Think of a situation when you severely neglected one of the four intelligences for a time. What impact did that situation have on the other three capacities?

________________________________________________________

________________________________________________________

________________________________________________________

________________________________________________________

________________________________________________________

________________________________________________________

________________________________________________________

________________________________________________________

________________________________________________________

## Developing Physical Intelligence—PQ

Self-assess how well you are currently developing your physical intelligence (body) by completing the table below. Key: 1 = never, 2 = seldom, 3 = often, 4 = usually, 5 = always.

| **Wise Nutrition** | **1** | **2** | **3** | **4** | **5** |
|---|---|---|---|---|---|
| 1. I eat a balanced diet that includes whole grains, fruits and vegetables and low-fat proteins. | | | | | |
| 2. I eat saturated fats and sugar sparingly. | | | | | |
| 3. I stop eating when I am satisfied (i.e., I avoid bingeing and overeating). | | | | | |
| 4. I drink six to ten eight-ounce glasses of water daily. | | | | | |
| 5. I take appropriate vitamins or supplements that I believe are healthful for my body. | | | | | |
| **Consistent, Balanced Exercise** | **1** | **2** | **3** | **4** | **5** |
| 6. I exercise a minimum of three times per week. | | | | | |
| 7. My weekly exercise routine includes stretching and flexibility. | | | | | |
| 8. My weekly exercise routine includes strengthening. | | | | | |
| 9. My weekly exercise routine includes aerobics. | | | | | |
| **Proper Rest, Relaxation, Stress Management and Prevention Thinking** | **1** | **2** | **3** | **4** | **5** |
| 10. I get 6 to 8 hours of sleep each night. | | | | | |
| 11. I participate in relaxation activities weekly. | | | | | |
| 12. I proactively look for ways to eliminate negative stress from my life. | | | | | |
| 13. I get annual health checkups. | | | | | |
| 14. I am aware of my genetic health predisposition. | | | | | |

Think about your current work situation. Do you feel fairly compensated?

________________________________________

________________________________________

________________________________________

________________________________________

________________________________________

________________________________________

________________________________________

How could you improve your physical work environment to promote greatness?

________________________________________

________________________________________

________________________________________

________________________________________

________________________________________

________________________________________

________________________________________

**Developing Mental Intelligence—IQ**

Self-assess how well you are currently developing your mental intelligence (mind) by completing the table below. Key: 1 = never, 2 = seldom, 3 = often, 4 = usually, 5 = always.

| **Continuous, Systematic, Disciplined Study and Education** | **1** | **2** | **3** | **4** | **5** |
|---|---|---|---|---|---|
| 1. I read at least one book each month. | | | | | |
| 2. I read articles from either newspapers or magazines regularly. | | | | | |
| 3. I avoid watching inane television programs or mindlessly surfing the Internet. | | | | | |
| 4. I take notes when listening to a speaker or reading something new. | | | | | |
| 5. I participate in classes of any kind that increase my knowledge. | | | | | |
| **Cultivation of Self-Awareness** | **1** | **2** | **3** | **4** | **5** |
| 6. I use the space between stimulus and response to pause and then take action. | | | | | |
| 7. I put my thoughts into writing for the purposes of examining, observing and changing myself. | | | | | |
| 8. I seek and encourage feedback from people in my personal and professional lives. | | | | | |
| 9. I pray, meditate or ponder regularly. | | | | | |
| **Learning by Teaching and Doing** | **1** | **2** | **3** | **4** | **5** |
| 10. I share my thoughts and feelings with people who are close to me. | | | | | |
| 11. I have meaningful conversations each week about things I am learning or thinking about. | | | | | |
| 12. I have a goal-planning system in place that allows me to apply what I learn. | | | | | |

What are you really good at?

What opportunities do you see for growth and development?

**Developing Emotional Intelligence—EQ**

Self-assess how well you are currently developing your emotional intelligence (heart) by completing the table below. Key: 1 = never, 2 = seldom, 3 = often, 4 = usually, 5 = always.

| **Self-Awareness** | **1** | **2** | **3** | **4** | **5** |
|---|---|---|---|---|---|
| 1. I believe I am free to choose and am responsible for my choices. | | | | | |
| 2. I use the space between stimulus and response to pause and respond based on my values and principles. | | | | | |
| 3. I use proactive language (e.g., "I control my feelings," "I choose," "I prefer," versus "He makes me so mad," "I can't" or "I have to"). | | | | | |
| 4. I spend my time and energy focused on things I can influence rather than on things I can do nothing about. | | | | | |
| **Personal Motivation** | **1** | **2** | **3** | **4** | **5** |
| 5. I envision and plan for outcomes before I act. | | | | | |
| 6. I live by a personal mission statement. | | | | | |
| 7. My mission and goals motivate and excite me each day to achieve greatness. | | | | | |
| **Self-Regulation** | **1** | **2** | **3** | **4** | **5** |
| 8. I focus on top priorities, which may or may not be urgent priorities. | | | | | |
| 9. I avoid the unimportant activities. | | | | | |
| 10. I have a planning system that allows me to execute my top priorities each day and each week. | | | | | |
| 11. I renew myself weekly to avoid burnout and stress. | | | | | |
| **Empathy** | **1** | **2** | **3** | **4** | **5** |
| 12. I listen with the intent to understand, not with the intent to reply. | | | | | |
| 13. I try to see things from the other person's perspective. | | | | | |
| 14. I avoid judging or advising when listening. | | | | | |

| Social Skills | 1 | 2 | 3 | 4 | 5 |
|---|---|---|---|---|---|
| 15. I seek mutual benefit for myself and others—win-win solutions. | | | | | |
| 16. I balance courage with consideration in my social interactions. | | | | | |
| 17. I value and celebrate the difference of others. | | | | | |
| 18. I practice creative cooperation to find the best solution. | | | | | |
| 19. I can express myself in a positive, productive way. | | | | | |

What have you always loved doing?

_______________________________________________

_______________________________________________

_______________________________________________

_______________________________________________

_______________________________________________

What opportunities are you passionate about?

_______________________________________________

_______________________________________________

_______________________________________________

_______________________________________________

_______________________________________________

_______________________________________________

**Developing Spiritual Intelligence—SQ**

Self-assess how well you are currently developing your spiritual intelligence (spirit) by completing the table below. Key: 1 = never, 2 = seldom, 3 = often, 4 = usually, 5 = always.

| **Integrity** | **1** | **2** | **3** | **4** | **5** |
|---|---|---|---|---|---|
| 1. I know what my personal values are. | | | | | |
| 2. I live my personal values. | | | | | |
| 3. I keep the promises I make to others. | | | | | |
| 4. I keep the promises I make to myself. | | | | | |
| **Meaning and Voice** | **1** | **2** | **3** | **4** | **5** |
| 5. I have a Personal Mission Statement that inspires me. | | | | | |
| 6. My work excites and challenges me. I love what I do. | | | | | |
| 7. My work allows me to be a whole person (using all four intelligences). | | | | | |
| 8. I am living my life's mission and calling each day. | | | | | |

What would make your days and weeks more meaningful to you?

______________________________________________

______________________________________________

______________________________________________

______________________________________________

______________________________________________

______________________________________________

What contribution would you love to make in your current roles?

______________________________________________

______________________________________________

______________________________________________

______________________________________________

______________________________________________

______________________________________________

## VIEWING THE FILM *A.B. Combs Elementary*

After you view the film *A.B. Combs Elementary* on your companion DVD or online, answer the following questions.

Who are some people in your life who acted as surrogate parents to you?

______________________________________________

______________________________________________

______________________________________________

______________________________________________

______________________________________________

______________________________________________

In thinking about these people, what did they inspire in you? What new direction or insights did they give you? What parts of your voice did they bring out in you?

______________________________________________________________

______________________________________________________________

______________________________________________________________

______________________________________________________________

______________________________________________________________

______________________________________________________________

What character principles would you like to strengthen in your life to help you discover or reaffirm your voice?

______________________________________________________________

______________________________________________________________

______________________________________________________________

______________________________________________________________

______________________________________________________________

______________________________________________________________

______________________________________________________________

How could introducing character principles at work or at home help others to find their voices?

______________________________________________________________

______________________________________________________________

______________________________________________________________

______________________________________________________________

______________________________________________________________

______________________________________________________________

## APPLYING YOUR KNOWLEDGE

Complete some or all of the following activities throughout the month to apply this concept to your personal and professional lives.

- Look back at the self-assessment scores from the "Developing Physical Intelligence—PQ" exercise. Select one area in which you scored yourself the lowest. Write this goal on your weekly or daily task list in your personal planning system. Commit to working on this area for the month to develop your body. *Remember, assume you've had a heart attack; now live accordingly.*

- Look back at the self-assessment scores from the "Developing Mental Intelligence—IQ" exercise. Select one area in which you scored yourself the lowest. Write this goal on your weekly or daily task list in your personal planning system. Commit to working on this area for the month to develop your mind. *Remember, assume the half-life of your profession is two years; now prepare accordingly.*

- Look back at the self-assessment scores from the "Developing Emotional Intelligence—EQ" exercise. Select one area in which you scored yourself the lowest. Write this goal on your weekly or daily task list in your personal planning system. Commit to working on this area for the month to develop your heart. *Remember, assume that everything you say about another can be heard by that person; now speak accordingly.*

- Look back at the self-assessment scores from the "Developing Spiritual Intelligence—SQ" exercise. Select one area in which you scored yourself the lowest. Write this goal on your weekly or daily task list in your personal planning system. Commit to working on this area for the month to develop your spirit. *Remember, assume you have a one-on-one visit with your Creator every quarter; now live accordingly.*

- Read *The Power of Full Engagement* by Jim Loehr and Tony Schwartz.

- Teach the main ideas of this chapter to at least two other people. List their names.

______________________________________________

______________________________________________

- Report your results to friends, colleagues and family members. List their names.

______________________________________________

______________________________________________

______________________________________________

______________________________________________

*Chapter* 5

# EXPRESS YOUR VOICE—VISION, DISCIPLINE, PASSION AND CONSCIENCE

*Before you begin this section of the workbook, read pages 64–93 in* The 8th Habit, *review the underlying principles listed here or read the summary in the Appendix.*

> *He that would govern others first should be master of himself.*
>
> —PHILLIP MASSINGER

## REVIEWING THE UNDERLYING PRINCIPLES

- Great leaders and achievers have the ability to manifest their four intelligences in the following ways: *vision* (mental), *discipline* (physical), *passion* (emotional), and *conscience* (spiritual).
- *Vision* is imagining a new future for yourself—one that taps into your own unique mission and role in life.
- *Discipline* is making the vision a reality. It's the hard work, persistence and willpower needed to achieve what you've imagined. Discipline is sacrificing something immediate and short-term for something lasting and long-term.
- *Passion* is the fire within that helps you stay disciplined even when things get hard. It is the wood that fuels the fire of the vision.
- *Conscience* is the moral voice within that allows you to realize the vision while staying true to your principles and values. Conscience is

the encouraging, directing guidance system that leads you to your highest and best use of vision, discipline and passion.

- Finding and expressing your voice means living as a whole person: body, mind, heart and spirit.

| WHOLE PERSON | 4 NEEDS | 4 INTELLIGENCES / CAPACITIES | 4 ATTRIBUTES | VOICE |
|---|---|---|---|---|
| BODY | To Live | Physical Intelligence (PQ) | Discipline | Need ("See"meeting needs) |
| MIND | To Learn | Mental Intelligence (IQ) | Vision | Talent (Disciplined focus) |
| HEART | To Love | Emotional Intelligence (EQ) | Passion | Passion (Love to do) |
| SPIRIT | To Leave a Legacy | Spiritual Intelligence (SQ) | Conscience | Conscience (Do what's right) |

## LEARNING OBJECTIVES

If you study and apply the underlying principles in this chapter for a month, you can expect to:

- Define or affirm your vision or dreams you have for your life.
- Understand the discipline it takes to achieve your personal vision.
- Improve in an area of your life in which you have lacked discipline.
- List the things you are passionate about—things that drive you.
- Acknowledge and listen to your conscience more closely.
- Create an action plan to find your voice (by combining your passion, talents and conscience with a need you perceive) in a specific role in your life.

## UNDERSTANDING YOUR VISION

The word *vision* means seeing the possibilities in people, projects, causes, departments and so on. Vision is a future state inspired by your voice.

Describe what you perceive as your vision for your life. Imagine that you are at a family gathering for your eightieth birthday party. Family, friends and colleagues have come to honor you.

What are the feelings in the room? ______________________________

______________________________________________________________

______________________________________________________________

______________________________________________________________

______________________________________________________________

______________________________________________________________

______________________________________________________________

What are the relationships like? _________________________________

______________________________________________________________

______________________________________________________________

______________________________________________________________

______________________________________________________________

______________________________________________________________

What have you shared together?

What tribute statements would your family give you?

What tribute statements would your friends give you?

________________________________________

________________________________________

________________________________________

________________________________________

________________________________________

________________________________________

________________________________________

________________________________________

What tribute statements would your colleagues give you?

________________________________________

________________________________________

________________________________________

________________________________________

________________________________________

________________________________________

________________________________________

Condense this information into several statements that represent the vision for your life.

______________________________________________________

______________________________________________________

______________________________________________________

______________________________________________________

______________________________________________________

______________________________________________________

______________________________________________________

Answer the following questions about your life vision.

| | **Circle One** | |
|---|---|---|
| Does it tap into your voice, your energy, your unique talent? | Yes | No |
| Does it give you a sense of *calling*, a cause worthy of your commitment? | Yes | No |
| Does your vision enable you to rise above your memory and help you see the unseen potential in other people? | Yes | No |
| Is your vision more than just getting things done or accomplishing some task? | Yes | No |
| Does your vision help you see people through the lens of their potential and their best actions rather than through the lens of their current behavior or weaknesses? | Yes | No |
| Does it generate positive energy and reach out and embrace others? | Yes | No |

## DEFINING DISCIPLINE

The word *discipline* means to sacrifice or delay something immediate for something better later on. Discipline is paying the price to bring the vision into reality.

Consider again this passage from *The 8th Habit*:

> Can you play the piano? I can't. I don't have the freedom to play the piano. I never disciplined myself. I preferred playing with friends to practicing as my parents and piano teacher wanted me to do. I don't think I ever envisioned myself as a piano player. I never had a sense of what it might mean, a kind of freedom to create magnificent art that might be valuable to me and to others throughout my entire life.

What skills do you possess because you used discipline to cultivate them?

________________________________________________

________________________________________________

________________________________________________

________________________________________________

What skills could you have that you don't have now simply because you lacked discipline? Describe your experience.

________________________________________________

________________________________________________

________________________________________________

Revisit the vision statement you wrote. What about the vision will take discipline to achieve?

______________________________________________________________

______________________________________________________________

______________________________________________________________

______________________________________________________________

______________________________________________________________

______________________________________________________________

## DEFINING PASSION

The word *passion* means the fire, the desire, the strength of conviction and the drive that sustains the discipline to achieve the vision.

What keeps you at a task when everything else says, "quit"? What are some of your passions?

______________________________________________________________

______________________________________________________________

______________________________________________________________

______________________________________________________________

______________________________________________________________

What do you feel is your special role and purpose in the world?

Describe a time when you were passionate about a project—something so compelling and absorbing that you could hardly think of anything else.

*When you can give yourself to work that brings together a need, your talent, and your passion, power will be unlocked.*

## DISCOVERING CONSCIENCE

The word *conscience* means the inner voice, the sense of right and wrong and the drive toward meaning and service. It is the guiding force to vision, discipline and passion.

Reread the following quote: "That you may retain your self-respect, it is better to displease the people by doing what you know is right than to temporarily please them by doing what you know is wrong."

Describe a time when you found yourself in this situation. What was the long-term outcome?

______________________________

______________________________

______________________________

______________________________

______________________________

______________________________

______________________________

______________________________

______________________________

______________________________

______________________________

Revisit the vision statement you just wrote. Conscience provides the *why* of your vision. Describe the conscience reflected in your vision.

______________________________________________

______________________________________________

______________________________________________

______________________________________________

______________________________________________

______________________________________________

______________________________________________

## VIEWING THE FILM *Stone*

After you view the film *Stone* on your companion DVD or online, answer the following questions.

How did Stone overcome his cultural overlay toward revenge by tapping into his birth-gifts?

______________________________________________

______________________________________________

______________________________________________

______________________________________________

______________________________________________

How did Stone personally pay the price in sacrifice and discipline?

______________________________________________________________________

______________________________________________________________________

______________________________________________________________________

______________________________________________________________________

______________________________________________________________________

How did Stone, with unrelenting passion, reach out to the young men in his country? What were the outcomes?

______________________________________________________________________

______________________________________________________________________

______________________________________________________________________

______________________________________________________________________

______________________________________________________________________

Think about a situation when you were intentionally or unintentionally hurt or limited like Stone. Describe that situation.

______________________________________________________________________

______________________________________________________________________

______________________________________________________________________

What choices did you make to handle the situation? Did you use your birth-gifts, or did you allow revenge and bitterness to control your actions?

____________________________________________________

____________________________________________________

____________________________________________________

____________________________________________________

____________________________________________________

____________________________________________________

____________________________________________________

____________________________________________________

Were you able to forgive in this situation? ______________________

____________________________________________________

____________________________________________________

How did forgiving or not forgiving impact your life? _______________

____________________________________________________

____________________________________________________

____________________________________________________

In thinking about your birth-gifts, what can you still do now about this situation?

## PART 1: FINDING YOUR VOICE SUMMARY

What are your highest values?

______________________________________________

______________________________________________

______________________________________________

What principles of effective living are these values based on?

______________________________________________

______________________________________________

______________________________________________

______________________________________________

______________________________________________

______________________________________________

______________________________________________

1. In column 1, list several primary roles in your life (roles in your family, community or work).
2. In column 2, list the needs you sense you could meet in each of the roles. These needs could focus on community, church, neighborhood, work, family, and so on.
3. In column 3, list the talents you posses that could meet the needs you listed.
4. In column 4, place a check mark in each row that you feel truly passionate about.
5. In column 5, place a check mark in each row where your conscience—your deep inner self—is promoting you to take action.

6. Place a star next to the rows in which the need you see intersects with your talents, passion and conscience.

| Roles | Needs | Talents | Passion | Conscience |
|---|---|---|---|---|
| 1. | | | | |
| 2. | | | | |
| 3. | | | | |
| 4. | | | | |
| 5. | | | | |
| 6. | | | | |

Imagine that you use your voice to take action in those areas by which you placed a star, then picture yourself once again at your eightieth birthday party. What will be your legacy in these areas?

_______________________________________________

_______________________________________________

_______________________________________________

_______________________________________________

_______________________________________________

_______________________________________________

_______________________________________________

_______________________________________________

_______________________________________________

_______________________________________________

_______________________________________________

_______________________________________________

_______________________________________________

_______________________________________________

_______________________________________________

## APPLYING YOUR KNOWLEDGE

Complete some or all of the following activities throughout the month to apply this concept to your personal and professional lives.

- Think more deeply about your unique purpose and role in life. Write down the vision or dreams you have for yourself, however improbable they seem now, in the journal for this chapter at the back of this workbook.

> *Down deep in every human heart is a hidden longing, impulse, and ambition to do something fine and enduring.*
>
> —GRENVILLE KLEISER

- Consider an area in your life in which you have lacked discipline. Commit to be more persistent this month in working on that area. Remember, sometimes it's mind over mattress. Help yourself stay committed by linking to your underlying purpose.

- Think about the things you are passionate about—the things that drive you. Write down those things in the journal for this chapter at the back of this workbook.

- Your conscience speaks to you all of the time. Perhaps yours has been telling you to improve in some way or make up for previous wrongs. Choose one thing that your conscience has been nagging you about and resolve it.

- Refer to the "Part 1: Finding Your Voice Summary" exercise on page 66 of this workbook. Develop the following action plan based on your answers.

| **Role** | | |
|---|---|---|
| **The need I see that taps into my passion and aligns with my conscience:** | | |
| **The talents I possess to fill the need:** | | |
| **ACTION PLAN: Outline the steps you will take to begin to fulfill the need and find your voice for this role.** | | |
| **Steps** | **By when?** | **Accountable to whom?** |
| 1. | | |
| 2. | | |
| 3. | | |
| 4. | | |
| 5. | | |
| 6. | | |

- Teach the main ideas of this chapter to at least two other people. List their names.

______________________________________________

______________________________________________

______________________________________________

- Report your results to friends, colleagues and family members. List their names.

______________________________________________

______________________________________________

______________________________________________

______________________________________________

______________________________________________

*Chapter* 6

# INSPIRING OTHERS TO FIND THEIR VOICE—THE LEADERSHIP CHALLENGE

*Before you begin this section of the workbook, read pages 97–123 in* The 8th Habit, *review the underlying principles below or read the summary in the Appendix.*

> *In everyone's life, at some time, our inner fire goes out. It is then burst into flame by an encounter with another human being. We should all be thankful for those people who rekindle the inner spirit.*
>
> —Albert Schweitzer

## REVIEWING THE UNDERLYING PRINCIPLES

- *Leadership* is communicating to people their worth and potential so clearly that they come to see it in themselves. The most common way of communicating this message to other people is through an organization.
- An *organization* is nothing more or less than a relationship with a purpose (its voice). You probably belong to many organizations. Marriages, families, community and volunteer groups, sports teams and businesses are all organizations. *In this workbook, the word organization refers to all the organizations you belong to, not just your work.*
- The highest challenge inside any organization is to set it up and run it in a way that enables each person to inwardly sense his or her worth and potential for greatness and to contribute his or her voice to accomplish the organization's purpose. This is the *Leadership Challenge.*

- Organizations require both management and leadership. *Either without the other is insufficient.*
- You *manage* and control things, but you must *lead* people. You manage things such as inventory, costs, systems, processes, physical resources, information, time, and so on, because they don't have the power and freedom to choose. (Remember my painful lesson that I needed management expertise from others to make FranklinCovey profitable. I couldn't lead inventory—it had to be managed.)
- The key to understanding organizational behavior is to study and understand human nature—to understand the *Whole-Person Paradigm* (body, mind, heart and spirit).
- Significant problems cannot be solved with quick-fix programs of the month. You must comprehend *the nature and root of the problems* you face.
- There are *two kinds of problems: chronic* (long-lasting, persistent) and *acute* (critical).

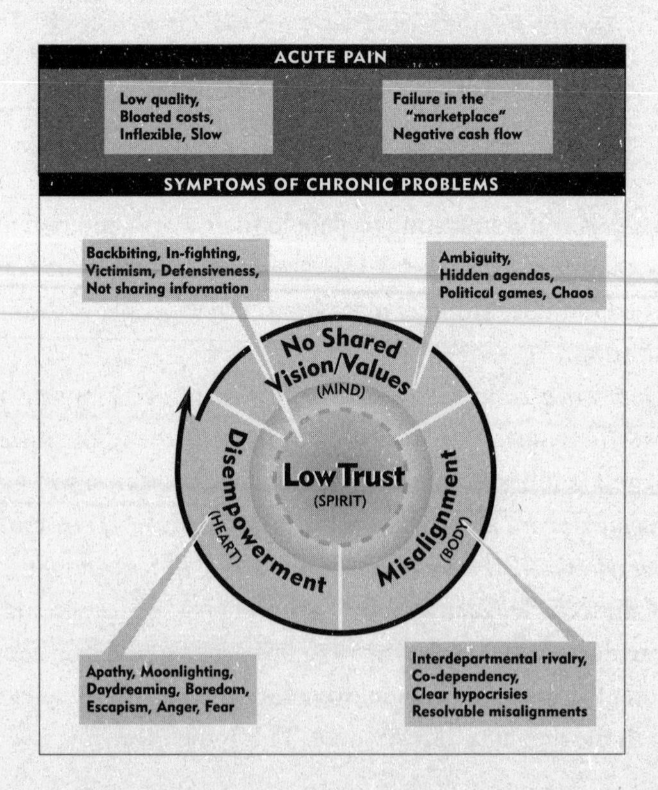

- Begin by addressing the symptoms of the chronic problems in your organization. In business, you cannot succeed with stockholders until you first succeed in the marketplace, and you can never succeed in the marketplace until you first succeed in the workplace. In the family, you cannot succeed with other family members until you succeed with yourself.
- The Industrial Age response to chronic problems is for the boss to make rules, increase control and demand greater efficiency. The Knowledge Worker Age response is to apply the 4 Roles of Leadership.

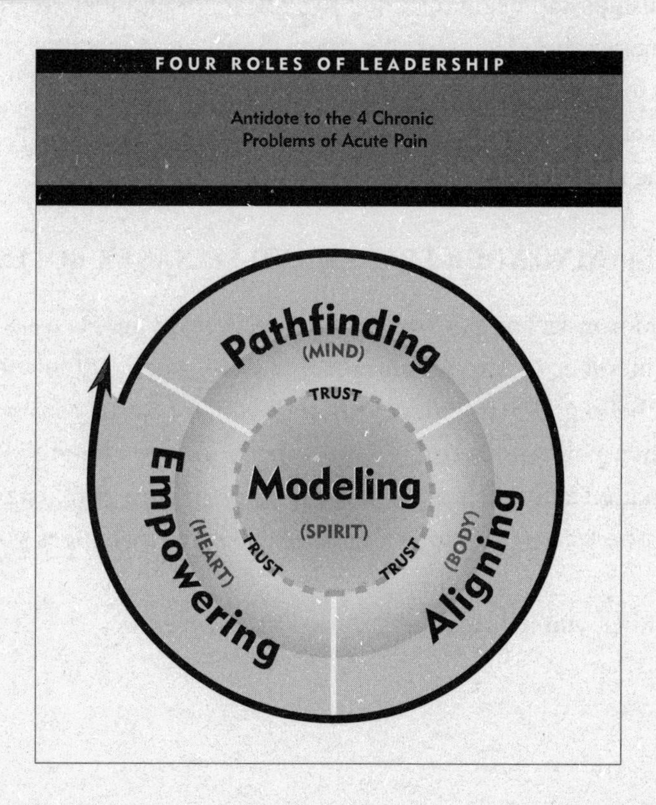


- The four roles help you inspire others to find their voices and achieve organizational greatness. Doing this can be summarized in two words: *Focus* and *Execution*. You will explore these processes in depth in the remainder of this workbook.

## LEARNING OBJECTIVES

If you study and apply the underlying principles in this chapter for a month, you can expect to:

- Know when to manage and when to lead.
- Understand how to increase your own influence and the influence of your organization (family, volunteer group, work, church, etc.).
- Be able to distinguish between chronic and acute problems.
- Identify chronic problems that apply to your organization and/or relationships and begin planning to alleviate or eliminate them.
- Understand the effects of the seven global seismic shifts and be able to form effective responses.
- Understand how applying the 4 Roles of Leadership will increase your focus and execution.

## DEFINING YOUR LEADER AND MANAGER ROLES

List the major tasks you perform in a typical week. Choose tasks you perform as a member of any organization (family, work, volunteer, etc.) to which you belong. Then indicate whether you are acting as a *manager* or a *leader* when you complete the task. Finally, review the table and consider if you are leading when you should be managing or managing when you should be leading. If so, indicate what behavior changes you should make.

Remember, you manage things; you lead people.

| Task | Leading or managing? | Is this the right choice? | What changes should you make? |
|---|---|---|---|
| | | | |
| | | | |
| | | | |
| | | | |
| | | | |
| | | | |

## UNDERSTANDING LEADERSHIP AND MANAGEMENT

Think of a boss you've had who was especially good at managing, but lacked leadership ability. How did you feel when working for him or her? What was your workplace like? What kind of results did your team achieve or fail to achieve?

______________________________________________

______________________________________________

______________________________________________

______________________________________________

______________________________________________

______________________________________________

Now think of a boss you've had who was especially good at leading, but lacked management ability. How did you feel when working for him or her? What was your workplace like? What kind of results did your team achieve or fail to achieve?

______________________________________________

______________________________________________

______________________________________________

______________________________________________

______________________________________________

Who do you know who is good at both managing and leading? How did you feel when working with him or her? What was your workplace like? What kind of results did your team achieve or fail to achieve?

____________________________________________________________

____________________________________________________________

____________________________________________________________

____________________________________________________________

____________________________________________________________

____________________________________________________________

____________________________________________________________

____________________________________________________________

## MEETING THE LEADERSHIP CHALLENGE IN YOUR ORGANIZATIONS

An *organization* is nothing more or less than a relationship with a purpose (its voice). Marriages, families, community, spiritual and volunteer groups, sports teams, businesses and so on are all organizations.

List some of the organizations to which you belong in the left column.

The highest challenge inside any organization is to set it up and run it in a way that enables each person to sense his or her innate worth and potential for greatness and to contribute his or her voice to accomplish the organization's purpose. This is the *Leadership Challenge.*

In the right column, write down ideas for ways in which you can respond to the Leadership Challenge for each organization you listed.

| Organizations to Which You Belong | How can you respond to the Leadership Challenge as a member of this organization? |
| --- | --- |
| | |
| | |
| | |
| | |
| | |
| | |
| | |

## UNDERSTANDING THE EFFECTS OF THE SEVEN GLOBAL SEISMIC SHIFTS

Review the seismic shifts information shown on pages 103–105 in *The 8th Habit,* then complete the following table. This exercise may require you to do additional research or work with people from your team.

| Seismic Shift | How does this affect your team? | What are some possible responses? |
|---|---|---|
| The globalization of markets and technologies | | |
| The emergence of universal connectivity | | |
| The democratization of information/expectations | | |
| An exponential increase in competition | | |
| The movement of wealth creation from financial capital to intellectual and social capital | | |
| Free agency | | |
| Permanent whitewater | | |

## VIEWING THE FILM *Permanent Whitewater*

After you view the film *Permanent Whitewater* on your companion DVD or online, answer the following questions.

What are the three constants we can rely on in dealing with challenges?

As a leader, what would it take for you to prepare someone on your team to deal with a whitewater-type environment? For example, what kind of judgment would this person need? Skills? Training? Flexibility? Relationships? Trust? Tools?

______________________________________________

______________________________________________

______________________________________________

## PREDICTING FOUR CHRONIC PROBLEMS AND THEIR SYMPTOMS

Having a Whole-Person Paradigm of human nature gives you an uncommon ability to explain, predict and diagnose the greatest problems in your life and in your department or team. When leaders possess inaccurate and incomplete paradigms of human nature, they design systems (i.e., communication, recruiting, reward and compensation and training) that fail to draw out the full potential of people. These systems misalign with the department's, team's or family's core mission, values and strategy.

On the chart below, circle the symptoms of chronic problems you see in your department or team.

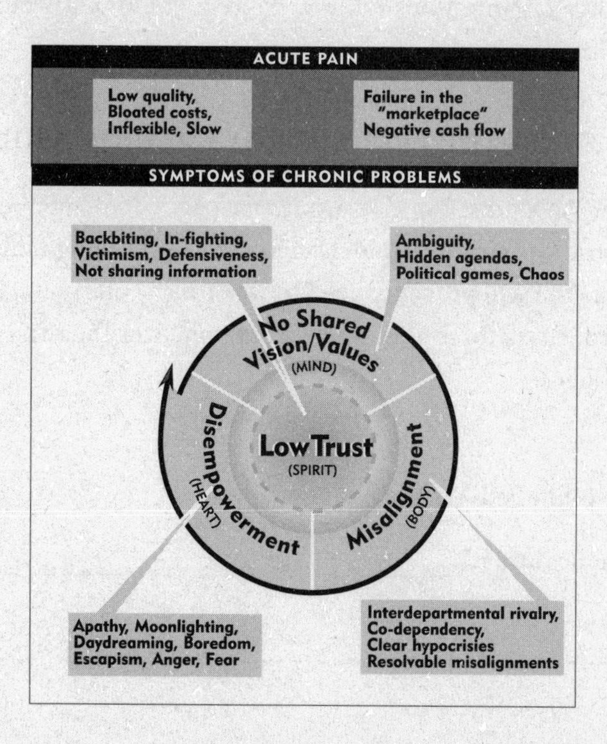

Each of the symptoms corresponds to one of the 4 Roles of Leadership. Complete the table below to identify the antidote to the problems.

| Whole-Person Paradigm | Symptoms of Chronic Problems | Chronic Problems | The 4 Roles of Leadership Antidote |
|---|---|---|---|
| Mind | | No shared vision/values | |
| Body | | Misalignment | |
| Heart | | Disempowerment | |
| Spirit | | Low trust | |

You have now identified the problems your department or team faces. You will learn more about what you can do to address these problems in later chapters.

Using a different colored pen or pencil, you can also complete this exercise for other organizations (family, church, community, etc.) to which you belong.

## UNCOVERING THE REAL COST OF CHRONIC PROBLEMS

Please review Appendix 4 in *The 8th Habit*, pages 365–368, before beginning. For those symptoms you identified in the preceding table, complete the following. You will probably need to work with colleagues, do some research or form a task force and dig deeply to uncover the real costs of each of these problems.

**Problem: No Shared Vision/Values**

How do you measure it?____________________________________

______________________________________________________

What is it now?

What would you like it to be?

What's the value of the difference?

Over time?________________________________________

________________________________________________

________________________________________________

________________________________________________

**Problem: Misalignment**

How do you measure it?________________________________

________________________________________________

________________________________________________

________________________________________________

What is it now?______________________________________

________________________________________________

________________________________________________

________________________________________________

What would you like it to be?____________________________

________________________________________________

________________________________________________

________________________________________________

What's the value of the difference? ______________________

______________________

______________________

______________________

Over time? ______________________

______________________

______________________

______________________

**Problem: Disempowerment**

How do you measure it? ______________________

______________________

______________________

______________________

______________________

What is it now? ______________________

______________________

______________________

What would you like it to be?

What's the value of the difference?

Over time?

**Problem: Low Trust**

How do you measure it?

What is it now? ________________________________________________

________________________________________________________________

________________________________________________________________

________________________________________________________________

What would you like it to be? __________________________________

________________________________________________________________

________________________________________________________________

________________________________________________________________

________________________________________________________________

What's the value of the difference? _____________________________

________________________________________________________________

________________________________________________________________

________________________________________________________________

Over time? _____________________________________________________

________________________________________________________________

________________________________________________________________

________________________________________________________________

## APPLYING YOUR KNOWLEDGE

Complete some or all of the following activities throughout the month to apply this concept to your personal and professional lives.

- Complete the "Uncovering the Real Cost of Chronic Problems" exercise for your team. Commit to sharing your results with key stakeholders in your department. Track your progress and planning in the journal at the end of this workbook.
- Complete the "Understanding the Effects of the Seven Global Seismic Shifts" exercise. Commit to sharing your results with key stakeholders in your team. Track your progress in the journal at the end of this workbook.
- Look at your answers to the exercise "Viewing the Film *Permanent Whitewater*." Develop an action plan to empower the person you thought of in that exercise to deal with the whitewater he or she faces.
- Read *Results Based Leadership* by Dave Ulrich, Jack Zenger, and Norm Smallwood.
- Read *The World Is Flat: A Brief History of the Twenty-First Century* by Thomas L. Friedman.
- Think of someone you know who hasn't found his or her voice. Keep this person in mind as you work through the remainder of this workbook. Try to help this person find his or her voice.
- Teach the main ideas of this chapter to at least two other people. List their names.

___________________________________________

- Report your results to friends, colleagues and family members. List their names.

___________________________________________

___________________________________________

*Chapter* 7

# THE VOICE OF INFLUENCE—BE A TRIM-TAB

*Before you begin this section of the workbook, read pages 126–145 in* The 8th Habit, *review the underlying principles listed here or read the summary in the Appendix.*

> *A trim-tab leader is constant—like a lighthouse, not a weathervane—a constant dependable source of light, not someone that twists and turns with every social wind.*

## REVIEWING THE UNDERLYING PRINCIPLES

- *Modeling* is the spirit and center of any leadership effort. Modeling is primarily done during or before the other three roles (pathfinding, aligning and empowering).
- To be a model you will need to *practice these four behaviors*:
  - Be a trim-tab (discussed in this chapter).
  - Be trustworthy: character and competence (discussed in Chapter 8).
  - Build trust (discussed in Chapter 9).
  - Search for the Third Alternative (discussed in Chapter 10).
- *Trustworthy people* (models or trim-tabs) can be easily identified because others within the organization seek their opinions, respect their input and value their experience.
- Modeling is not just the work of individuals; it's also the work of teams. A *complementary team* is one that builds on each individual's

strengths and organizes to make individual weaknesses irrelevant.

- Your *voice of influence* is how you respond to the inner desire to make a difference—to matter, to extend your influence. It is an attitude you have and a choice you make.
- The *Greek Philosophy of Influence* is an excellent summary of the process of increasing your voice of influence. *Ethos* is your ethical self—the part of you that models trustworthiness and builds trust. *Pathos* is your empathetic self—the part of you that seeks to understand others. *Logos* is your logical self—the part of you that seeks to be understood by others.
- A *trim-tab* is the small rudder that turns the big rudder that turns the ship. Trim-tab leaders spread their influence no matter what position they hold. Trim-tab leaders consistently exercise initiative by making positive, effective choices.

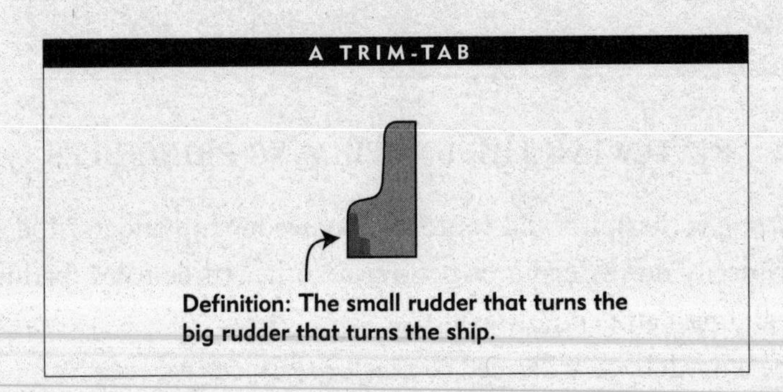


- Your *Circle of Concern* consists of those things that concern and interest you (overall organizational policy and leadership, the stock market, politics, etc.). Your Circle of Influence® consists of those things you have direct influence or control over (your personal productivity, your team or department, your savings and spending, how you vote, etc.).
- The 7 Levels of Initiative shown here depicts the choices available to you when you are assigned any task. You choose which level of

initiative to use based on how far the task lies within or outside your Circle of Influence.

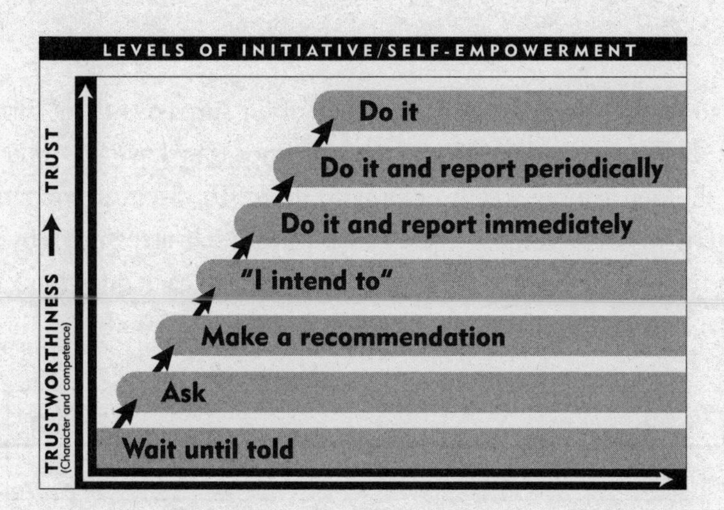


- It takes judgment and wisdom to know what level of initiative to exercise—what you should do, how you should do it when you should do it and perhaps most important, why you should do it. If you choose wisely, little by little, your Circle of Influence will expand because you will have built trust with other people.

## LEARNING OBJECTIVES

If you study and apply the underlying principles in this chapter for a month, you can expect to:

- Understand the importance of modeling.
- Learn how to work within your Circle of Influence.
- Make choices based on the 7 Levels of Initiative.
- Determine what your level of influence currently is and how to expand it.
- Learn how to become a trim-tab, why it is important and how to apply the skills.

- Practice pathos.
- Diagnose the five cancerous behaviors and how to respond.

## EXAMINING YOUR INFLUENCE

Trim-tab leaders exercise influence that often surpasses their formal authority. They can be identified by the influence they have on other people within the department, team or organization. To discover what trim-tab characteristics you have, complete the following self-assessment by placing an X in the box that best represents your answer to each question.

Key: 1 = never, 2 = seldom, 3 = often, 4 = usually, 5 = always.

| | 1 | 2 | 3 | 4 | 5 |
|---|---|---|---|---|---|
| Is your opinion sought? | | | | | |
| Describe an example that supports the rating you gave yourself. | | | | | |
| Is your input respected? | | | | | |
| Describe an example that supports the rating you gave yourself. | | | | | |
| Is your experience valued? | | | | | |
| Describe an example that supports the rating you gave yourself. | | | | | |

| | 1 | 2 | 3 | 4 | 5 |
|---|---|---|---|---|---|
| Are you involved in setting strategic direction for your department or team? | | | | | |
| Describe an example that supports the rating you gave yourself. | | | | | |
| Do you strongly identify with the vision of your department or team? | | | | | |
| Describe an example that supports the rating you gave yourself. | | | | | |
| Does your team build on each individual's strengths and organize to make weaknesses irrelevant? | | | | | |
| Describe an example that supports the rating you gave yourself. | | | | | |

Don't worry if you answered no to some questions. The exercises in this workbook are designed to help you fill in any gaps you may have.

You may also want to complete this questionnaire for your family or other organization.

**DRAWING ON THE POWER OF INFLUENCE**

Describe a situation in which you felt like you were a victim of a bad boss, hopeless relationship or unbearable situation.

Reread this quote: "Victimism gives your future away." Why did you feel like a victim in this situation?

How could you have better chosen your response to the other person's behavior?

_______________________________________________

_______________________________________________

_______________________________________________

_______________________________________________

_______________________________________________

_______________________________________________

_______________________________________________

## BECOMING A TRIM-TAB

Be sensitive, be wise and be careful regarding timing and approach, but do something about your situation. Avoid complaining, criticizing or being negative; be especially wary of absolving yourself from responsibility and simply blaming "them" for failures.

Reread the story of the Twenty Group on pages 130–131 in *The 8th Habit*. These general agents were able to exercise their moral authority to initiate change. However, they could do this only because they first had ethos—they were trustworthy and had credibility.

Becoming a trim-tab requires ethos—credibility. Think of your team, department or family. Place an X on the line to represent the level of ethos (trustworthiness and credibility) you believe you have. (To help you self-assess, think about your answers to the previous exercise "Examining Your Influence.")

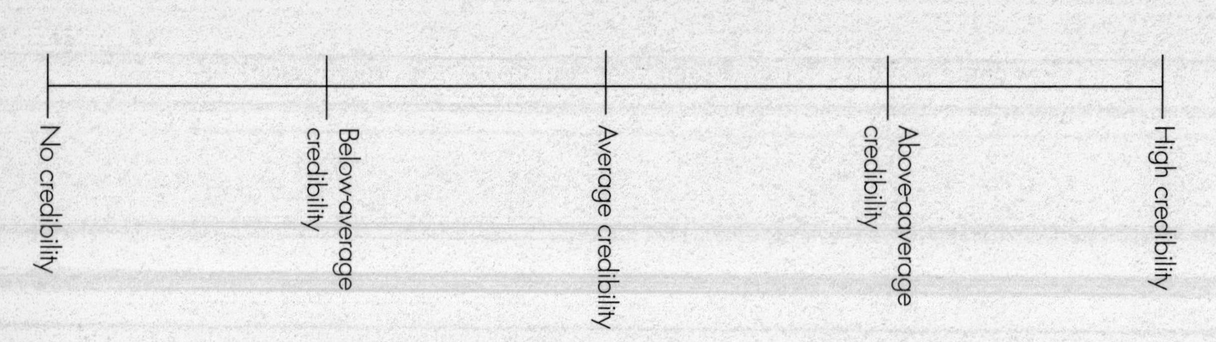


If you marked anywhere from average and below, what are some things you can do to become more trustworthy, build trust and gain credibility with this group?

______________________________________________

______________________________________________

______________________________________________

______________________________________________

______________________________________________

______________________________________________

______________________________________________

______________________________________________

______________________________________________

______________________________________________

______________________________________________

If you marked anywhere from average and above, you are ready to take the next step.

What are some issues you would like to address in your team, department or family? Describe them here.

Of the issues you listed, place an X through the ones far outside your Circle of Influence.

Of the issues you listed, circle the ones that are within your Circle of Influence. Choose one in particular.

For the issue you chose, who are the stakeholders or decision makers?

______________________________________________

______________________________________________

______________________________________________

______________________________________________

______________________________________________

For the issue you chose, who could help you work on the problem? (Remember to choose someone who also has high ethos—trustworthiness, trust and credibility.)

______________________________________________

______________________________________________

______________________________________________

______________________________________________

______________________________________________

______________________________________________

How will you demonstrate pathos to these stakeholders or decision makers? In other words, what will you say to show them that you truly understand their point of view on this issue?

______________________________

______________________________

______________________________

______________________________

______________________________

______________________________

______________________________

______________________________

______________________________

______________________________

Once the decision makers feel understood, how will you demonstrate logos? What plan do you want to put forth? What solutions will you propose to meet the specific challenges of making a change?

______________________________

______________________________

______________________________

After you approach the stakeholders or decision makers, record what happened in your journal at the back of this workbook. Record what went well and what could go better next time.

Repeat the process for another item within your Circle of Influence that you circled on the previous page.

## PRACTICING ETHOS, PATHOS, LOGOS

Think of a conflict or problem you are having with another person, either personally or professionally.

1. Use the space below to describe to the best of your ability how the other person sees the issue and why he or she feels and thinks that way. Describe the person's feelings, concerns and ultimate goals.

2. If possible, share what you have written with the other person. Confirm that you understand the issue from his or her point of view. Be sure the person feels completely understood before you proceed to the next step.
3. Present your thoughts on the issue. Work with the other person to see if you can come to a synergistic solution to the problem that meets both your needs.
4. Record the results in your journal at the end of this workbook. Did the process produce the desired results or at least an improvement? Did you build a stronger relationship with the other person? Will you practice this technique again?

## UNDERSTANDING THE 7 LEVELS OF INITIATIVE OR SELF-EMPOWERMENT

You choose which level of initiative to use based on how far the task lies within or outside your Circle of Influence. By exercising a level of initiative, you can change the nature of a job you do not enjoy, or you can influence others that are in your Circle of Influence.

In the table below, describe the pros and cons for each level. Think about the appropriateness of each level in different situations. Think about which levels are based on the Whole-Person Paradigm. (For definitions of each level, see pages 133–140 in *The 8th Habit*.)

| **Level of Initiative or Self-Empowerment** | **Pros/Cons** |
|---|---|
| Wait until told. | Pros:<br><br>Cons: |
| Ask. | Pros:<br><br>Cons: |
| Make a recommendation. | Pros:<br><br>Cons: |
| "I intend to." | Pros:<br><br>Cons: |
| Do it and report immediately. | Pros:<br><br>Cons: |
| Do it and report periodically. | Pros:<br><br>Cons: |
| Do it. | Pros:<br><br>Cons: |

## DIAGNOSING THE FIVE CANCEROUS BEHAVIORS

Does your department, team or family *regularly* exhibit any of the 5 Cancerous Behaviors? In the figure shown below, circle all those that apply.

**FIVE CANCEROUS BEHAVIORS**

- **Criticizing**
- **Complaining**
- **Comparing**
- **Competing**
- **Contending**

Do you regularly engage in any of these behaviors? If yes, which one?

________________________________________

________________________________________

How do others react to you when you engage in one of these behaviors?

________________________________________

________________________________________

________________________________________

________________________________________

________________________________________

How do you react when others engage in one of these behaviors?

_______________

_______________

_______________

_______________

_______________

If you did not circle any of the behaviors—congratulations! If you did, don't worry. Faithfully completing and applying the practices in this workbook over the course of the year will help you eliminate or reduce these cancerous behaviors.

## VIEWING THE FILM *Mauritius*

After you view the film *Mauritius* on your companion DVD or online, answer the following questions.

How did this country and society trim-tab its own success in spite of ethnic, racial and cultural differences? What did they do?

_______________

_______________

_______________

_______________

What was their result?______________________________________

How do the organizations to which you belong compare to Mauritius?

What principles from the video could you apply to improve the effectiveness of the organizations to which you belong?

## APPLYING YOUR KNOWLEDGE

Complete some or all of the following activities throughout the month to apply this concept to your personal and professional lives.

- Every day, you are faced with small moments of choice at work and at home in which you can become a trim-tab. Work to apply the trim-tab spirit in your work and your personal life. Model the behaviors you would like to see in others and observe and record the effects in your journal at the back of this workbook.

- Throughout the coming month, be on the lookout for the five cancerous behaviors (criticizing, complaining, comparing, competing and contending) in yourself and in others. Observe the effects of these behaviors and make a conscious effort to avoid them and to encourage others to avoid them. Techniques might include changing the subject, pointing out how harmful negativity is to the department or team, and sharing the story of the trim-tab with others and encouraging them to practice the trim-tab spirit. Record your observations in your journal at the back of this workbook.

- Share the trim-tab story with your family and work team and encourage everyone to practice the trim-tab spirit. Consider establishing a trim-tab award (an anchor, compass, rudder, toy boat and so on would be appropriate symbols) and ask your group to nominate people for the trim-tab award. Encourage multiple winners!

- When you are given an assignment or hear about a challenge facing your team, consider it with the 7 Levels of Initiative in mind. What level of action is appropriate? Is this an instance in which you can stretch your boundaries effectively? What is the best you can do under the circumstances?

- Review your answers to the "Becoming a Trim-Tab" exercise on page 136. Work toward changing the issue you listed in that exercise.

- Read *On Becoming a Leader* by Warren Bennis.

- Teach the main ideas of this chapter to at least two other people. List their names.

_______________________________________________

_______________________________________________

- Report your results to friends, colleagues and family members. List their names.

_______________________________________________

_______________________________________________

_______________________________________________

_______________________________________________

*Chapter* 8

# THE VOICE OF TRUSTWORTHINESS—MODELING CHARACTER AND COMPETENCE

*Before you begin this section of the workbook, read pages 146–160 in* The 8th Habit, *review the underlying principles listed here or read the summary in the Appendix.*

> *Ninety percent of all leadership failures are character failures.*

## REVIEWING THE UNDERLYING PRINCIPLES

- To be a model you need to practice these four behaviors:
  - Be a trim-tab (discussed in Chapter 7).
  - Be trustworthy: character and competence (discussed in this chapter).
  - Build trust (discussed in Chapter 9).
  - Search for the Third Alternative (discussed in Chapter 10).
- Trust is the glue that holds together teams and relationships. *Trust is shared and reciprocated* between people.
- You *merit trust* by both giving trust and acting with integrity.
- Trustworthiness comes from *character* and *competence*.
- *Character* consists of:
  - *Integrity*: You keep promises made to yourself and others.
  - *Maturity*: You combine courage and compassion.

- *Abundance Mentality:* You see life as a vast array of different opportunities, wealth and resources and not as a competition with only one winner.
- *Competence* consists of:
  - *Technical*: The skills and knowledge necessary to complete a task.
  - *Conceptual*: The ability to see the big picture—to think strategically, not just tactically.
  - *Interdependency*: The knowledge that the parts affect the whole—that all of life is interconnected.
- Wisdom and judgment occur when character and competence intersect.
- You cannot make significant progress in your relationships if your own life is a mess or if you are untrustworthy. *To improve any relationship, you must start with yourself.*
- Modeling means living the 7 Habits of Highly Effective People. This phrase summarizes the first three habits: *Make and keep promises.* The next three habits are summarized by the phrase: *Involve people in the problem and work out the solution together.* The final habit is renewing your spirit and character and the spirit and character of your complementary team.

**PRINCIPLES AND PARADIGMS EMBODIED IN THE 7 HABITS**

| *Habit* | *Principle* | *Paradigm* |
|---|---|---|
| **❶ Be Proactive** | **Responsibility/Initiative** | **Self-determination** |
| **❷ Begin with the End in Mind** | **Vision/Values** | **Two Creations / Focus** |
| **❸ Put First Things First** | **Integrity/Execution** | **Priority / Action** |
| **❹ Think Win-Win** | **Mutual Respect/Benefit** | **Abundance** |
| **❺ Seek First to Understand, Then to be Understood** | **Mutual Understanding** | **Consideration Courage** |
| **❻ Synergize** | **Creative Cooperation** | **Value Differences** |
| **❼ Sharpen the Saw** | **Renewal** | **Whole Person** |

- The 7 Habits are character principles that shape *who and what you are*. The 4 Roles of Leadership (modeling, pathfinding, aligning and empowering) are *what you do* as a leader to inspire others to find their voices.
- Because modeling is the first of the four roles, your first job is to *get your act together*. To decide what matters most to you and to ensure that you focus relentlessly on those things and those things only.
- Your tool for becoming a model for others is a *personal planning system.*
- Begin by identifying your *mission* and governing *values*. Then identify your most important *roles* (as a friend, co-worker, family member, etc.).
- Set *goals* every week that are aligned with these values and roles.
- Complete weekly planning by planning your big rocks for the week. *Big rocks* are those things that matter most in your life.
- *Plan daily* by making realistic task lists, prioritizing tasks and scheduling appointments.

## LEARNING OBJECTIVES

If you study and apply the underlying principles in this chapter for a month, you can expect to:

- Understand and begin to practice the behaviors required for modeling.
- Learn and apply the three facets of personal character.
- Learn and apply the three facets of competence.
- Identify roles and big rocks, and learn how to set and complete goals.
- Practice daily and weekly planning to improve your effectiveness and focus.
- Write your Personal Mission Statement.

## LIVING THE FACETS OF PERSONAL TRUSTWORTHINESS

Remember that trustworthiness is composed of character and competence.

### Character

Rate yourself on how well you are currently living the three facets of personal character—integrity, maturity and the Abundance Mentality—by placing an X in the box that best describes you.

Key: 5 = I consistently demonstrate this trait, 4 = Most of the time I demonstrate this trait, with a few exceptions, 3 = Sometimes I demonstrate this trait, but it is in less than half of my interactions, 2 = Once in a while I remember to demonstrate this trait, 1 = I rarely, if ever, demonstrate this trait.

| | 1 | 2 | 3 | 4 | 5 |
|---|---|---|---|---|---|
| Integrity: Keeping promises to self and others; aligning with principles and natural laws that ultimately govern positive consequences | | | | | |
| Maturity: Having integrity; having courage and consideration in dealing with tough issues | | | | | |
| Abundance Mentality: Seeing life as a cornucopia with abundant resources, opportunities and wealth | | | | | |

Now let's look at the competence side of personal trustworthiness.

**Competence**

Rate yourself on how well you are currently living technical competence, conceptual knowledge and interdependency by placing an X in the box that best describes you.

Key: 5 = This is a skill I possess and consistently demonstrate, 4 = Most of the time I use this skill, with a few exceptions, 3 = Sometimes I use this skill, but it is in less than half of my interactions, 2 = Once in a while I remember to use this skill, 1 = I rarely, if ever, demonstrate this trait.

| | 1 | 2 | 3 | 4 | 5 |
|---|---|---|---|---|---|
| Technical competence: Having the skill and knowledge to accomplish a particular task | | | | | |
| Conceptual knowledge: Being able to see the big picture—how all of the parts relate to one another; thinking strategically | | | | | |
| Interdependency: Realizing that all of life is connected | | | | | |

Trustworthiness is the confidence you and others have in your character and competence. To lead in the twenty-first century you will be required to have both.

## VIEWING THE FILM *Big Rocks*

This film demonstrates how we use our three birth-gifts—choice, principles and the four human intelligences—to create positive change in our lives.

After you view the film *Big Rocks* on your companion DVD or online, answer the following questions.

What are the big rocks in your life? ______________________

______________________

______________________

______________________

______________________

What are some of the small rocks? ______________________

______________________

______________________

______________________

______________________

What are the top three things that prevent you from focusing on your big rocks?

______________________

______________________

______________________

______________________

______________________

How could you eliminate these barriers to success? ________________

________________________________________________

________________________________________________

________________________________________________

________________________________________________

## APPLYING YOUR KNOWLEDGE

Complete the following activities throughout the month to apply this concept to your personal and professional lives.

- Refer to the "Living the Facets of Personal Trustworthiness" exercise on page 113. List any traits that you marked 3 or below.

________________________________________________

________________________________________________

- What will you commit to do to improve your scores in these areas? Track your progress using the journal at the back of this workbook.

________________________________________________

________________________________________________

________________________________________________

- If you do not already have a personal planning system, select either an electronic or paper-based system and begin using it. FranklinCovey.com or FranklinCovey retail stores have a selection of electronic and paper systems.

- Once you have your planning system, begin by writing down what matters most to you. Then build those governing priorities into your weekly and daily planning so you can effectively balance the need for structure and discipline with spontaneity, focus and execution.
  - It takes 21 days to form a habit. Commit to regularly using the personal planning system you select for at least 21 days.
  - Read *First Things First* by Stephen R. Covey, Rebecca Merrill and Roger Merrill.
  - Read *The 7 Habits of Highly Effective People* by Stephen R. Covey.
  - Write your Personal Mission Statement by completing the Mission Statement formulator at *www.The8thHabit.com*. Click on The 8th Habit, then click on Book Tools.

- Teach the main ideas of this chapter to at least two other people. List their names.

________________________________________

________________________________________

- Report your results to friends, colleagues and family members. List their names.

________________________________________

________________________________________

________________________________________

________________________________________

*Chapter* 9

# THE VOICE AND SPEED OF TRUST

*Before you begin this section of the workbook, read pages 161–185 in* The 8th Habit, *review the underlying principles listed here or read the summary in the Appendix.*

> *It is a greater compliment to be trusted than to be loved.*
>
> —George MacDonald

## REVIEWING THE UNDERLYING PRINCIPLES

- *Trust is the glue of life.* It is the glue that holds departments, teams and relationships together.
- A lack of trust is the very definition of a bad relationship. When trust is high, *relationships and communication are easy and effortless.* Mistakes are forgiven. When trust is low, relationships are difficult and communication often fails.
- Trust in a relationship is not a constant. It must be maintained and actively nurtured by making regular deposits in the *Emotional Bank Accounts* of others. The Emotional Bank Account is like a financial bank account into which you make emotional deposits and withdrawals.
- Deposits are based on principles central to human relationships. Applying these principles and making deposits requires three things. They require that you practice:

- Initiative
- Humility
- Sacrifice

**The Ten Deposits**

- *Seeking First to Understand:* You must understand the other person's frame of reference before you can know what constitutes a real deposit to them. (Recall the story in *The 8th Habit* of the woman who thought a clean house would be a deposit to her husband but learned that it was not something he really cared about.)
- *Making and Keeping Promises:* Promise-keeping is hard—that is why nothing destroys trust faster than breaking a promise, and nothing builds trust faster than keeping a promise. Do not take promise-making lightly.
- *Honesty and Integrity:* You cannot be trustworthy without actively demonstrating that you are honest and have integrity.
- *Kindness and Courtesies:* People have feelings that must be acknowledged and honored. Small courtesies and kindness yield huge dividends.
- *Thinking Win-Win or No Deal:* Win-lose thinking is the underlying assumption of almost all negotiations and problem solving and, while it is appropriate in some competitive situations, when applied to all situations it becomes manipulative and self-defeating. Thinking win-win or no deal means that you agree either to find a solution that is a true win for you and a true win for the other person or you agree to part ways. Win-win thinking requires a willingness to sacrifice—to suspend your own interests long enough to understand what the other person wants most.
- *Clarifying Expectations:* If you study the underlying roots of almost all communication breakdowns or broken relationships, you'll find they come from either ambiguous or broken expectations around

roles and goals: who does what and why. It is a simple thing to clarify expectations with family and co-workers, but it will yield important results.

- *Being Loyal to Those Not Present:* This is one of the most difficult deposits and is a true test of your character. The next time you are tempted to gossip, it may help to reflect that how you talk about someone in his or her absence communicates to others in the room how you will talk about them in their absence.
- *Apologizing:* A sincere apology requires you not only to say the words "I'm sorry," but to demonstrate that you are sorry by your actions and to avoid justifying your behavior (in other words, you don't say or think, "I'm sorry, but . . .").
- *Giving and Receiving Feedback:* It may seem odd to think of giving feedback (especially if it is negative) as a deposit but, while it is one of the most difficult communications, it is also one of the most needed. The best way to give feedback is to describe your concerns and feelings about the situation rather than label or blame the other person. When you receive feedback, express gratitude for it (even if it hurts). Remember, we all need feedback, particularly about our blind spots.
- *Forgiving:* True forgiveness requires that you forget, let go and move on. Forgiving releases your negative energy and puts you back in control of your emotions. Remember that no one can do you harm without your consent.

Finally, remember that trust is also a verb. It requires that you actively practice trusting and affirming the people around you—your family, friends and co-workers.

## LEARNING OBJECTIVES

If you study and apply the underlying principles in this chapter for a month, you can expect to:

- Understand the importance of trust in departments, teams and relationships, and learn how to improve trust.
- Improve your relationships by making deposits in others' Emotional Bank Accounts.
- Work to achieve win-win solutions with other people.
- Have the tools to improve your relationships with people with whom you share low trust.
- Understand the significance of making and keeping promises.

## CONSIDERING HIGH- AND LOW-TRUST RELATIONSHIPS

List two to three people with whom you have a high-trust relationship and two to three people with whom you have a low-trust relationship.

| High-Trust Relationship | Low-Trust Relationship |
|---|---|
| | |
| | |
| | |

List the common characteristics of the people with whom you share a high-trust relationship. Attempt to uncover what about these people, or what about you in relation to these people, makes the relationship high trust.

Now do the same for the people with whom you share a low-trust relationship.

How do you behave when you are around the high-trust people and the low-trust people?

| High-Trust Behaviors | Low-Trust Behaviors |
|---|---|
| | |

What do you think would be the result if you started treating the low-trust people with high-trust behaviors (and vice versa)?

______________________________________________

______________________________________________

______________________________________________

______________________________________________

______________________________________________

______________________________________________

No relationship is one-sided. You may have very good reasons why you have a low-trust relationship with another person; however, if you want to change the relationship to one of high trust, you will have to change your behaviors. One option is to practice applying the high-trust/deposit behaviors to the low-trust people and observing the results.

## MAKING DEPOSITS INTO THE EMOTIONAL BANK ACCOUNT

List below several things you could do that would be a deposit into another person's Emotional Bank Account. Remember, it is only a deposit if the other person views it as one.

| With whom do you have an important relationship in your life? | What deposit could you make into his or her Emotional Bank Account this week? | What sacrifice will it require of you to make this deposit? |
|---|---|---|
| | | |
| | | |
| | | |
| | | |
| | | |

## REFLECTING ON YOUR PROMISES

It's easy to make a promise; we probably make several promises a day without thinking. It usually quickly satisfies other people, especially when they are stressed or anxious about something they need you to fix.

Think back on the past five days. Have you made any promises to people? List them here.

| What is the promise you made? | To whom? | What have you done to keep that promise? | What will happen to the relationship if you do not keep the promise? Describe the results. |
|---|---|---|---|
| 1. | | | |
| 2. | | | |
| 3. | | | |
| 4. | | | |
| 5. | | | |

## THINKING WIN-WIN OR NO DEAL

Win-win agreements can be developed between any two parties (manager/associate, parent/child, client/supplier, etc.). Choose a relationship or situation that could benefit from a win-win solution and answer the questions that follow.

| **Name(s):** | |
|---|---|
| **Situation:** | |
| **What's a win for you?** | **What's a win for him or her?** |
| | |

You will use this table later in the "Applying Your Knowledge" section.

## REFLECTING ON NEEDED APOLOGIES

To learn to say, "I was wrong; I'm sorry," then live accordingly, is one of the most powerful ways to build trust and relationships.

How do you typically react when someone sincerely apologizes to you?

________________________________________

________________________________________

________________________________________

________________________________________

Think of three relationships in your life that would be built or strengthened if you sincerely apologized for a past wrong. List them here.

| Relationship | Past Wrong | How could the relationship grow if I made a sincere apology? |
|---|---|---|
| Example:Our proofreader, Irene | I showed several co-workers in staff meeting some errors that Irene had missed. Irene heard my comments and we no longer speak to each other. | We could let go of burdensome ill feelings and begin to foster a team spirit again. I could use her skills on several projects, and I could become a resource on her projects again. |
| | | |
| | | |
| | | |

## VIEWING THE FILM *Teacher*

As you view the film *Teacher* on your companion DVD or online, think about the following points.

- Study the film through the lens of the two roads—the upper road to greatness and the lower road to mediocrity.
- Study how through her choices, Anne Sullivan became a person of vision, discipline and passion, governed by conscience and the moral authority that developed within her through sacrificing and overcoming adversity.
- Study how the relationship of trust between Helen and Anne formed through constant deposits: the speedy subtle communication that occurred; the patience, persistence and understanding; and the bonding that took place.
- Reflect on how Anne found her own voice and devoted her life to inspiring others (Helen) to find theirs.

## APPLYING YOUR KNOWLEDGE

Complete some or all of the following activities throughout the month to apply this concept to your personal and professional lives.

- Refer to the list of people with whom you have a low-trust relationship you created on page 121 in this workbook. Commit yourself to building higher-trust relationships with these people by making regular deposits in their Emotional Bank Accounts. Record your results in your journal at the back of this workbook.

- Refer to the "Reflecting on Needed Apologies" exercise on page 127. Commit to ask sincerely for the forgiveness of the people you listed, and put the issue behind you.

- Complete a Win-Win Agreement. Make an appointment with the person you identified in the table on page 126 to seek a Win-Win or No-deal Agreement.

During the meeting, clarify the issues described in the Win-Win Agreement:

| **Win-Win Agreement** | |
|---|---|
| **Desired Results** | What is the end in mind? What are the outcomes we want? |
| **Guidelines** | What rules do we follow? What are the guidelines for accomplishing the results? |
| **Resources** | What resources do I have to work with (e.g., people, money, tools, materials, technology)? |
| **Accountability** | How will we measure how well it's going? |
| **Consequences** | What are the rewards of achieving the outcome? What are the consequences of not achieving the outcome? |

Begin the meeting by practicing pathos (see page 102 in this workbook). Before you begin the Win-Win Agreement discussion, make sure you both completely understand the other person's position and are able to restate it to his or her satisfaction.

- Think of a relationship in your life that would benefit from clarifying roles and goals. Make an appointment with that person and walk through the following process together.
  - Obtain two flip charts. At the top of one flip chart write, "How you see MY roles and goals," and on the other write, "How you see YOUR roles and goals."
  - Invite the other person to think about the questions on the flip charts and list his or her answers. Do not reach any judgments, agreements or disagreements until you both feel the flip charts are adequately filled in or complete.

- Examine the flip charts to reveal any differing expectations. Brainstorm how you can close the gap between expectations and actual roles and goals.

- Read *Lead to Succeed* by Rick Pitino.

- Read *Gandhi, the Man* by Eknath Easwarn.

- Teach the main ideas of this chapter to at least two other people. List their names.

____________________________________________

____________________________________________

- Report your results to friends, colleagues and family members. List their names.

____________________________________________

____________________________________________

____________________________________________

____________________________________________

*Chapter* 10

# BLENDING VOICES—SEARCHING FOR THE THIRD ALTERNATIVE

*Before you begin this section of the workbook, read pages 186–214 in* The 8th Habit, *review the underlying principles listed here or read the summary in the Appendix.*

> *Creative thinking involves breaking out of established patterns in order to look at things in different ways.*
>
> —EDWARD DEBONO

## REVIEWING THE UNDERLYING PRINCIPLES

- The capacity and ability to produce a synergistic (creative interaction) Third Alternative is built upon the *foundation of moral authority and trust.*
- The Third Alternative is a better alternative than any that have been proposed. It's not your way or my way or a compromise; it is *a better solution.*
- Finding a Third Alternative requires creative effort and a willingness to really listen, search and be open. It requires a *win-win mind-set.*
- Many people think both people have to think win-win. Not so. *Only one person has to think win-win,* then prepare the other person to join by practicing empathy (understanding), seeking the other's interest and sticking with the process until the other person feels trust.

- To be the win-win thinker requires that you *work hard at the personal level* to overcome your insecurities and competitive feelings.
- *Communication* is the most important skill required in searching for the Third Alternative. In fact, it is the most important skill in life. To truly listen means to get out of your thoughts, your value system and your history and get deeply into the viewpoint of the other person. This is called *Empathic Listening.*

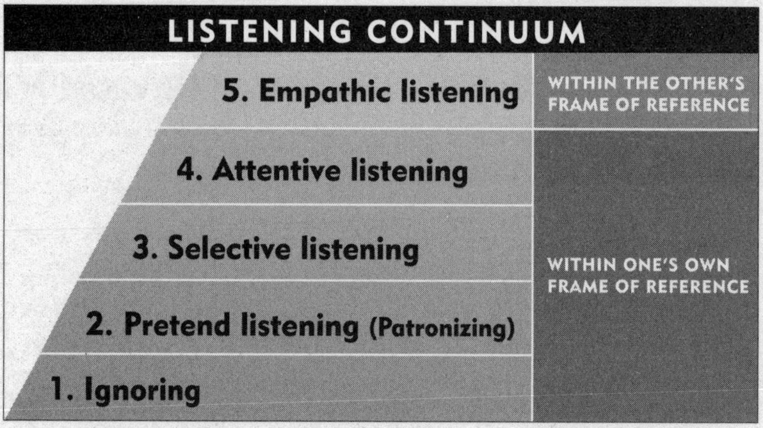

**LISTENING CONTINUUM**

|  |  |
|---|---|
| **5. Empathic listening** | WITHIN THE OTHER'S FRAME OF REFERENCE |
| **4. Attentive listening** | WITHIN ONE'S OWN FRAME OF REFERENCE |
| **3. Selective listening** | |
| **2. Pretend listening (Patronizing)** | |
| **1. Ignoring** | |

- There are four important things to know about communication.
  1. You have to be sincerely open and really listen to the other person.
  2. You do not see the world as it is; you see it as you are. Your interpretation of a situation colors your perception.
  3. There is more than one way to interpret something. The more you invest your ego in your perception, the less likely you will be to find a Third Alternative.
  4. Most communication breakdowns are a matter of semantics or perceptions. To eliminate this problem, listen with the other person's frame of reference.
- There are two steps to searching for a Third Alternative. These steps are not sequential. Sometimes you start with one, sometimes

with the other. These steps will only work if at least one of the parties is willing to approach the situation from a win-win perspective.

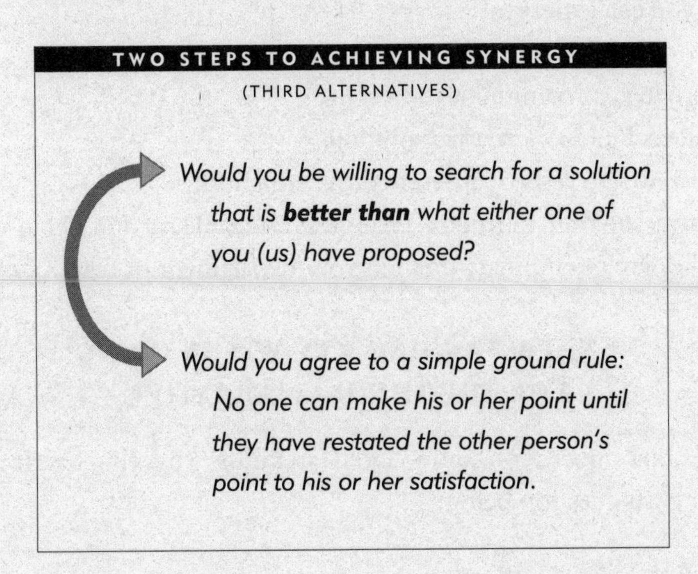


- Building a complementary team requires that you practice modeling open, Third Alternative communication. Leaders above all need to manifest the moral authority inherent in this kind of communication; however, it can begin at any level by those who practice open communication with co-workers, family members and others.
- There are four Bermuda Triangles that can lead to the decay and death of an idea.
    1. *Idea stage:* Killing a good idea because of negativity, doubt and fear.
    2. *Production stage:* Killing a great idea because of poor execution.
    3. *Management stage:* Management is unable or unwilling to establish systems to sustain and increase the production.
    4. *Change stage:* When the department or team gets so bogged down with its own bureaucratic life that it cannot respond to changing market conditions.

## LEARNING OBJECTIVES

If you study and apply the underlying principles in this chapter for a month, you can expect to:

- Improve your communication skills.
- Achieve Third Alternative solutions.
- Learn how to resolve differences synergistically.
- Identify the four Bermuda Triangles of idea decay and begin work to alleviate or eliminate them in your department or team.

## UNDERSTANDING WIN-WIN IN GOING FOR THE THIRD ALTERNATIVE

Let's see how much you know about attaining win-win. Circle True or False for each question below.

| | | |
|---|---|---|
| True | False | 1. Both people have to Think Win-Win. |
| True | False | 2. The other person has to cooperate initially. |
| True | False | 3. You must prepare the other person for win-win by practicing empathy or deep listening, seeking his or her interest and consistently staying with it until the other person feels trust. |
| True | False | 4. Win-win means compromise. |
| True | False | 5. Seeking a Third Alternative requires creativity. |
| True | False | 6. To understand does not mean to agree with. |

*Answers: 1. F, 2. F, 3. T, 4. F, 5. T, 6. T*

## OBTAINING THE SKILL SET TO REACH THE THIRD ALTERNATIVE

Recruit another person to do this experiment with you.

1. You (and only you) look at the picture on page 194 in *The 8th Habit* for one second.
2. Without looking at it yourself, let the other person see the picture on page 196 in *The 8th Habit*.
3. Both of you look at the picture on page 211 in *The 8th Habit*.
4. What do you both see in the final picture? A picture of a young lady or a saxophone player? Which of you is right?
5. Talk with the other person to understand what he or she sees. Listen carefully and try to see what he or she is seeing.
6. Once you understand the other person's point of view, explain yours to him or her. Help him or her see what you're seeing.

What accounted for your difference in perception?

______________________________________________

______________________________________________

What if you understood what the other person had seen before you gave your answer about what the picture was? How would this have changed your discussion?

______________________________________________

______________________________________________

______________________________________________

______________________________________________

How was conditioning at play here?

How is conditioning at play in our lives in regard to the Third Alternative?

*We do not see the world as it is;*
*we see the world as we are.*

## ASSESSING YOUR DEPARTMENT OR TEAM

Refer to the Bermuda Triangles information on pages 212–213 in *The 8th Habit*. Where do you think most ideas are killed in your department or team? (You can also think about this process as it applies to your family.)

| **Bermuda Triangles** | **Place a check mark if ideas within your department, team, or family are killed here.** | **Why?** |
|---|---|---|
| Idea stage | | |
| Production stage | | |
| Management stage | | |
| Change stage | | |

## VIEWING THE FILM *Street Hawkers*

As you view the film *Street Hawkers* on your companion DVD or online, answer the following questions.

In this case, mutual understanding led to a creative solution. How did this benefit both parties?

______________________________________________

______________________________________________

______________________________________________

______________________________________________

If the company had not applied Third Alternative thinking, what would have been the results for the organization and the street hawkers?

______________________________________________

______________________________________________

______________________________________________

______________________________________________

How do you think your department or team would have responded in a similar situation? Why?

______________________________________________

______________________________________________

---

---

## APPLYING YOUR KNOWLEDGE

Complete some or all of the following activities throughout the month to apply this concept to your personal and professional lives.

- Do the arm wrestle win-win thinking demonstration with your family or co-workers (see pages 188–191 in *The 8th Habit*). What did you learn? Record your thoughts in the journal at the back of this workbook.

- Identify an issue (either personal or professional) to which you would like to seek a Third Alternative solution. Perhaps you and your spouse are having a conflict about responsibilities around the home; perhaps you would like to seek a solution to your daughter's messy room or your son's less than stellar grades; perhaps you and another department have an ongoing conflict about processes or cost transfers. List the conflict here:

---

---

---

---

- Make an appointment with the other party(ies) to work through the two steps: Would you be willing to search for a solution that is better than either one of us proposed? Would you agree to a simple ground rule that no one can make his or her point until he or she has restated the other person's point to his or her satisfaction?

- Pick an object you would like to use as your talking stick (see pages 197–201 in *The 8th Habit)* and use it at your next family or department meeting. Explain how the talking stick is used and what results can be expected. Record your results in your journal at the back of this workbook.

- Refer to the "Assessing Your Department or Team" exercise on page 137. Consider what you could do to help steer your department, team or family safely out of danger. Record your thoughts in your journal at the back of this workbook.

- Read *Harvard Business Review on Effective Communication* by Ralph G. Nichols, et. al.

- Read *Listening: The Forgotten Skill: A Self-Teaching Guide* by Madelyn Burley-Allen.

- Teach the main ideas of this chapter to at least two other people. List their names.

______________________________________________

______________________________________________

- Report your results to friends, colleagues and family members. List their names.

______________________________________________

______________________________________________

______________________________________________

______________________________________________

*Chapter* 11

# ONE VOICE—PATHFINDING SHARED VISION, VALUES AND STRATEGY

*Before you begin this section of the workbook, read pages 215–230 in* The 8th Habit, *review the underlying principles here or read the summary in the Appendix.*

> *The very essence of leadership is that you have to have vision; you can't blow an uncertain trumpet.*
> *—Theodore M. Hesburgh, President, University of Notre Dame*

## REVIEWING THE UNDERLYING PRINCIPLES

- As a model, it is important for you to *show others* how a person who has found his or her voice fulfills the other three roles of a leader—pathfinding, aligning and empowering.
- Pathfinding means that you *unite people who are diverse in their strengths and perspectives into one voice and one great purpose.*
- When faced with a pathfinding challenge, you have three options:
    1. *Announce* the vision or strategy to your team without any involvement on their part.
    2. *Get bogged down* in paralysis by analysis and committee-itis instead of execution.
    3. If you have built a foundation of trust and are trustworthy yourself, you can reasonably involve key stakeholders in making the decision and *rely on the power of identification* to ensure the buy-

in of the other people in the organization. (This option is demonstrated by the Ritz-Carlton.)

- *Managers are typically better at modeling* than they are at providing focus and clear direction (pathfinding). The result is that people do not have a clear vision of how their work relates to the department's or team's key priorities.
- Pathfinding leaders seek to eliminate this problem by *providing order and focus.* Pathfinders clearly communicate key goals. Once people understand their goals and how they relate to the broader strategy, their commitment increases.
- Deciding on a strategy requires facing these realities:
    - *Market realities:* What is your market? Who is your competition? What are the industry trends and challenges?
    - *Core competencies:* What are you really good at? What do you really care about? What will people pay for? What does your conscience counsel?
    - *Stakeholder wants and needs:* Who are your target customers? What do they really want and need? What are their issues? What is the market reality of their industry?
    - *Values:* What are your stakeholder's values? What are your values? What is the central purpose of your department or team?
- Pathfinding can be the toughest of the four roles because you must deal with many personalities, agendas, trust levels and egos. Modeling is crucial to this role because it gives you credibility and encourages cooperative involvement. A team that identifies with the leader more easily trusts that the path set is the correct one.
- *Your tools* as a pathfinding leader are the mission statement and the strategic plan. Implementing these tools allows you to decide what to focus on as a department, team or family.
    - The *mission statement* includes the purpose, vision and values of your department, team or family.
    - The *strategic plan* is a concise description of how you will provide value. It's your focus.

- To unleash the power of your department, team or family, you need to *clarify its mission, vision and values* in a way that overlaps the four needs (body, mind, heart, and spirit) of the individuals who are members.
- Success requires *a balance between mission and margin.* Too much focus on either element is unhealthy—the key is balance.

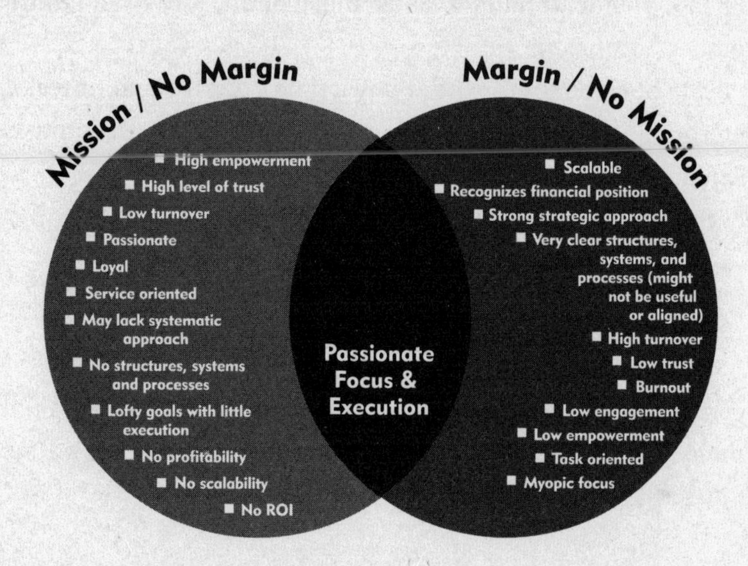


- In a sense, *any organization has only two roles: customers and suppliers.* The essence of good business, therefore, is the quality of the relationship between customer and supplier.
- *Executing the strategy* requires setting up the structure, getting the right people in the right jobs with the right tools and support, then getting out of the way and providing help when requested.
- One of the greatest challenges facing organizations, departments, teams and families is to translate the overall vision into *executable, measurable, line-of-sight goals* for everyone. Too often strategic plans are vague and leaders fail to convert them into near-term goals. Strategic goals should be few, prioritized, measurable and tracked via a compelling scoreboard.

## LEARNING OBJECTIVES

If you study and apply the underlying principles in this chapter for a month, you can expect to:

- Understand the purpose of the pathfinding role.
- Evaluate your pathfinding skills and identify areas for improvement.
- Evaluate how the four realities impact your department or team.
- Determine if your department or team balances between mission and margin.
- Develop a mission statement, values list and strategic plan.

## UNCOVERING YOUR PATHFINDING STRENGTHS AND WEAKNESSES

Managers are typically rated higher on their work ethic (modeling) than on their ability to provide clear direction and focus (pathfinding). Rate yourself on these pathfinding and co-missioning activities.

### Questionnaire 1 (for managers and team leaders)

Place a check mark in the column that best applies.

| | Never | Sometimes | Always |
|---|---|---|---|
| I provide team members and co-workers with clear, measurable, achievable goals. | | | |
| I make sure people understand their goals and are committed to them. | | | |
| I rate performance against a standard scoreboard. | | | |
| I make sure my team's goals are directly related to the organization's highest priorities. | | | |

For those questions to which you answered never or sometimes, commit to implementing a clear set of criteria that will provide focus for the group of people you lead.

### Questionnaire 2

Rate yourself on your understanding and commitment to your department or team goals by placing a check mark in the column that best applies.

| | **No** | **Somewhat** | **Yes** |
|---|---|---|---|
| I know my department's or team's mission statement. | | | |
| I understand my department's or team's strategic plan and why it was chosen. | | | |
| I am fully committed to achieving my department's or team's strategic plan. | | | |
| I understand how my work directly relates to achieving the strategic plan. | | | |

It is important that you understand and commit to the department's or team's mission and strategic plan. If you cannot or have not, why?

______________________________________________

______________________________________________

______________________________________________

______________________________________________

______________________________________________

______________________________________________

## UNDERSTANDING THE FOUR REALITIES

You must grapple with four realities (market realities, core competencies, stakeholder wants and needs and values) before you can fully comprehend and be prepared to execute the pathfinding role.

Before you can focus, you must clarify a few questions about each reality. Begin walking through the pathfinding process by answering the questions below for your department or team.

### Market Realities

How do people in your department or team perceive the marketplace?

___

___

___

What is the larger political, economic and technological context?

___

___

___

What are the competitive forces?

___

___

___

What are the trends and characteristics of the industry?

---

---

---

Are there looming disruptive or innovative technologies and/or business models that could make your entire industry obsolete?

---

---

---

**Core Competencies**

What are your department's or team's unique strengths?

---

---

---

---

---

---

What are the people deeply passionate about?

What will people pay for from your department or team?

What does your conscience counsel?

**Stakeholder Wants and Needs**

Who are your stakeholders—your target customers?

___

___

___

What do they really want and need?

___

___

___

What are their issues, problems and concerns?

___

___

___

What do their customers want and need?

___

___

___

What is the market reality of the industry in which they operate?

What possible technologies or business models could disrupt their business or make them obsolete?

What about the owners—those who have supplied the capital or paid the taxes—what are their wants and needs?

What about the associates, employees, co-workers—what are their wants and needs?

__________________________________________________

__________________________________________________

__________________________________________________

__________________________________________________

What about the suppliers, distributors and dealers—the entire supply chain?

__________________________________________________

__________________________________________________

__________________________________________________

__________________________________________________

What about the community and the natural environment?

__________________________________________________

__________________________________________________

__________________________________________________

__________________________________________________

__________________________________________________

**Values**

What are your department's or team's values?

What is the central purpose of the department or team?

What is its central strategy in accomplishing that purpose?

Do the department's or team's values align with the strategy?

How are those values prioritized in different contexts in times of stress and pressure?

## VIEWING THE FILM *Goal!*

As you view the film *Goal!* on your companion DVD or online, notice the similarities in the challenges you face at work in trying to get everyone focused on the same big goal.

What problems were making the children's soccer team ineffective?

Think about the statistics presented in the film. Do you know the key goals for your team or department? Do other people?

If you know the goals, are you passionate about them? Do other people on your team or in your department seem passionate about them?

Do you understand what you personally need to do to reach the key goals? Do other people seem to understand what they need to do?

______________________________________________________________

______________________________________________________________

## BALANCING MARGIN AND MISSION

Unless your department or team produces consistent profits over time, eventually you lose your opportunity to deliver on your mission. In the diagram below, circle the phrases that you believe apply to your department or team.

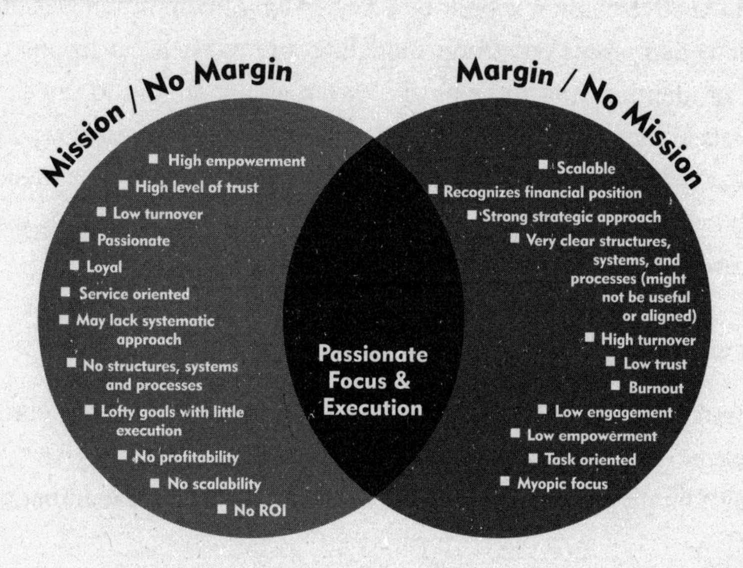


Is your enterprise in balance or did you circle more phrases in one circle than in another? The key is to find balance, since neither approach on its own is sustainable.

## DEVELOPING YOUR STRATEGIC PLAN

Pathfinding for a team or department is what modeling is for an individual. It's the ability to link what you're passionate about delivering to what your customers are passionate about receiving. To do this, you need to understand what matters most to your stakeholders (as you did in the last exercise), define your mission and values (if you have not done so already) and create a vision and strategy that link the two passions.

**Writing Your Team Mission Statement**

A mission statement should encompass your sense of purpose, vision and values. If your team or family has not already created its mission, vision and values, begin the process.

An effective mission is built by a key group of committed stakeholders who have demonstrated strong modeling and as such can count on the power of identification to bring the group along. If you do not feel that your stakeholder group has achieved this level of identification, you must develop a task force from all segments of the team to drive the mission, vision and values process. The work you did on the four realities is useful in this process.

**Developing Your Strategic Plan**

The strategic plan defines how you will provide value to your customers and stakeholders; it's your value proposition—your team's voice. (If you are creating a family strategic plan, your stakeholders are each member of your family.)

When creating your strategic plan, answer the following questions.

Who are your customers and stakeholders?

______________________________________________

______________________________________________

______________________________________________

Who do you want your customers and stakeholders to be?

________________________________________

________________________________________

________________________________________

What matters most to your stakeholders?

________________________________________

________________________________________

________________________________________

Is what matters most to the team what is most important to your stakeholders? Why or why not?

________________________________________

________________________________________

________________________________________

What valued service or product are you offering?

________________________________________

________________________________________

________________________________________

What is your plan, including deadlines, to achieve certain goals in getting and keeping customers?

| Plan | Deadline |
|---|---|
| 1. | |
| 2. | |
| 3. | |
| 4. | |
| 5. | |

## APPLYING YOUR KNOWLEDGE

Complete some or all of the following activities throughout the month to apply this concept to your personal and professional lives.

- Refer to the "Uncovering Your Pathfinding Strengths and Weaknesses" exercise on page 144 and review your responses. If you have not yet implemented clear measurable goals for your team members (or family members), begin to implement them over the next month. For Questionnaire 2, make sure to find the answers to any questions to which you answered "no" or "somewhat." Record your answers in the journal at the back of this workbook.

- Refer back to the "Balancing Margin and Mission" exercise on page 155. If any of the issues uncovered in that exercise fall within your Circle of Influence, plan to meet with other leaders and begin to achieve a mission/margin balance.

- Examine your team and/or department's mission, vision and values to determine if they meet the four needs (survival/body; growth and development/mind; relationships/heart; meaning, integrity and contribution/spirit). If they do not (and if it falls within your Circle of Influence), take steps to revise them to bring them into alignment.

- If you have not already done so, complete the process of creating your family's or team's mission, vision and values.

- Ask various people on your team (or family) to describe how what they do contributes to the overall strategic plan of the team. Record the results in your journal at the back of this workbook. Are there any patterns?

- Refer to the "Developing Your Strategic Plan" exercise on page 156. Over the next month, begin to implement the plan you outlined.

- Read *Good to Great* by Jim Collins.

- Teach the main ideas of this chapter to at least two other people. List their names.

________________________________________

________________________________________

________________________________________

________________________________________

- Report your results to friends, colleagues and family members. List their names.

____________________________________________

____________________________________________

____________________________________________

____________________________________________

*Chapter* 12

# THE VOICE AND DISCIPLINE OF EXECUTION—ALIGNING GOALS AND SYSTEMS FOR RESULTS

*Before you begin this section of the workbook, read pages 232–248 in* The 8th Habit, *review the underlying principles listed here, or read the summary in the Appendix.*

> *If you put good people in bad systems you get bad results.*
> *You have to water the flowers you want to grow.*

## REVIEWING THE UNDERLYING PRINCIPLES

- In the last chapter, you worked on defining the core values and priorities of your family, team or department. In this chapter, you will focus on alignment—on making sure that systems and structures reinforce the values and priorities you selected.
- The process of alignment may require a deep and sometimes frightening examination of many so-called sacred cows. People you included may be resistant to tackle established systems and traditions. The modeling and pathfinding skills you have developed will pave the way for this challenging work.
- Departments, teams or families whose systems do not align with their stated core values operate in an atmosphere of distrust. When leadership says one thing but does another, even trustworthy people find themselves in conflict with the department, team or family. One of the key results of alignment is trust.

- Alignment requires the discipline of walking your talk—making sure your processes, rewards and systems are in line with your vision and values.
- You are perfectly aligned to get the results you get. So if you are not getting the results you want, assume you are out of alignment. To get back on track, study the gap between the results you are getting and the results you want, and reward the behaviors that will give you those results.
- Examine the reward systems you have in place to ensure that you are not inadvertently rewarding behaviors you don't want. (Recall the company that wanted cooperation but rewarded competition.) If you want cooperation, institute a win-win system that rewards it. If you want your kid's room to stay clean, institute a win-win reward for that. If you want innovation—institute a win-win reward for new ideas. One way to achieve this is through the use of a balanced scorecard, which you will learn how to create in Chapter 14.
- Aligning is an ongoing process that requires constant monitoring and feedback. A pilot must constantly monitor his flight plan and make adjustments to keep the plane on the correct path. A leader must do the same.
- Aligning requires that you balance the production of desired results (the eggs) and the producer (the goose). If you kill the goose, you lose the capacity to produce more eggs. This means you must give as much attention to the capacity (the goose—or the relationships and people) as you give to the bottom-line results (the eggs—money, profits or a clean house).

## LEARNING OBJECTIVES

If you study and apply the underlying principles in this chapter for a month, you can expect to:

- Discover if your team, department or family is living in alignment with its stated values.
- Begin planning to bring your group into alignment.
- Analyze the six rights and discover if there are gaps between the results you want and the results you get.

## REFLECTING ON YOUR TEAM'S CURRENT ALIGNMENT

In the FranklinCovey xQ™ survey, only 48 percent of respondents agreed that their organizations generally live up to the stated values of the organization.

Circle always, sometimes or rarely in the following statements.

My family always/sometimes/rarely lives up to our values.

My team always/sometimes/rarely lives up to our values.

____________________ (insert department name) always/sometimes/rarely lives up to its values.

To bring a system into alignment, review the six rights (process, structure, people, information, decisions and rewards) as they apply to your team.

Answer these assessment questions.

| The current structures, systems and processes in our team: | **Circle One:** | |
|---|---|---|
| Enable people to execute top priorities. | Yes | No |
| Create roadblocks to executing top priorities. | Yes | No |
| Are consistent with the team's espoused values. | Yes | No |
| Foster sacred cows that do not align with our mission and strategic plan. | Yes | No |
| Encourage trust. | Yes | No |

Now take a deeper cut by answering the following survey as it applies to your work (your team, department, division, etc.).

Key: 1 = Poor, 2 = Fair, 3= Good, 4 = Very Good, 5 = Excellent.

| **Processes** | | | | | |
|---|---|---|---|---|---|
| Processes allow us to complete our work effectively and efficiently. | ① | ② | ③ | ④ | ⑤ |
| Outdated or unnecessary tasks are eliminated or redesigned. | ① | ② | ③ | ④ | ⑤ |
| Process steps are clear and repeatable. | ① | ② | ③ | ④ | ⑤ |
| The people using the processes are involved in any process redesign. | ① | ② | ③ | ④ | ⑤ |
| **Processes Total:** | | | | | |
| **Structure** | | | | | |
| Our structure (the roles on our team) ensures that we have the right knowledge, skills and expertise to be effective. | ① | ② | ③ | ④ | ⑤ |
| Reporting relationships are clear. | ① | ② | ③ | ④ | ⑤ |
| People are able to get work done without encountering excessive bureaucracy. | ① | ② | ③ | ④ | ⑤ |
| The structure of our work team allows us to work effectively with key stakeholders. | ① | ② | ③ | ④ | ⑤ |
| **Structure Total:** | | | | | |
| **People** | | | | | |
| Our selection process allows us to hire people who have both the right job skills and the right fit with our group. | ① | ② | ③ | ④ | ⑤ |
| We have effective systems in place to teach and train new people to meet changing job requirements. | ① | ② | ③ | ④ | ⑤ |
| People receive assignments that challenge their abilities and provide new learning. | ① | ② | ③ | ④ | ⑤ |
| Our systems make it easy for the right people to get new positions or promotions. | ① | ② | ③ | ④ | ⑤ |
| **People Total:** | | | | | |

| **Information** | | | | | |
|---|---|---|---|---|---|
| Needed information is accessible and usable. | ① | ② | ③ | ④ | ⑤ |
| Information flows first to the person who needs it most. | ① | ② | ③ | ④ | ⑤ |
| People are aware of work relevant to them that others are doing. | ① | ② | ③ | ④ | ⑤ |
| There is an effective system for sharing new learning. | ① | ② | ③ | ④ | ⑤ |
| **Information Total:** | | | | | |
| **Decisions** | | | | | |
| The people with the right knowledge and expertise are consulted on decisions. | ① | ② | ③ | ④ | ⑤ |
| Decisions are made based on the mission, values, vision and strategy. | ① | ② | ③ | ④ | ⑤ |
| Decisions are made in a timely way. | ① | ② | ③ | ④ | ⑤ |
| People are clear about who makes what decisions. | ① | ② | ③ | ④ | ⑤ |
| **Decisions Total:** | | | | | |
| **Rewards** | | | | | |
| People receive proper recognition for good work. | ① | ② | ③ | ④ | ⑤ |
| Poor work is addressed constructively. | ① | ② | ③ | ④ | ⑤ |
| People are paid fairly, relative to each other and the local market. | ① | ② | ③ | ④ | ⑤ |
| Rewards are determined according to what people say is important to them rather than arbitrarily chosen for them. | ① | ② | ③ | ④ | ⑤ |
| **Rewards Total:** | | | | | |

Which category scored the highest? ______________________

Which category scored the lowest? ______________________

What actions can you take within your Circle of Influence to help improve conditions in your lowest category?

______________________________________________________________________

______________________________________________________________________

______________________________________________________________________

______________________________________________________________________

______________________________________________________________________

______________________________________________________________________

______________________________________________________________________

______________________________________________________________________

______________________________________________________________________

## FOCUSING ON FAMILY RESULTS

Is there a gap between the results you want (homework, curfews, housework) and the results you are getting (poor grades, late nights, messy rooms)? If so, examine the reward systems you have in place.

What behaviors would you like to discourage?

______________________________________________________________________

______________________________________________________________________

_______________________________________________

_______________________________________________

What behaviors would you like to encourage?

_______________________________________________

_______________________________________________

_______________________________________________

_______________________________________________

What is the current reward structure, if any? (Note that ignoring a behavior is a type of reward.)

_______________________________________________

_______________________________________________

_______________________________________________

_______________________________________________

What should you change? Are you rewarding the right behaviors?

_______________________________________________

_______________________________________________

_______________________________________________

## FOCUSING ON TEAM RESULTS

The key to the principle of alignment is to always begin with the results. Ask yourself the following questions about your team.

What kind of results are you getting?

Are your stakeholders happy with the return on their investment?

What about team members? Are they happy with the return on their physical, emotional, mental and spiritual investment?

What about suppliers?

What about the community?

---

---

Do you have any sense of social responsibility toward children, schools, the streets, the air and water, the context in which your employees work and raise their families?

---

---

How do the results from your stakeholders, employees and customers benchmark against world-class standards?

---

---

---

## VIEWING THE FILM *Berlin Wall*

As you view the film *Berlin Wall* on your companion DVD or online, consider the following points.

- Remember how truly difficult it is for people to develop a new mind-set, paradigm, or different way of thinking, and how it requires a new skill-set and tool-set.
- Think about how futile it would be to teach people the new skills and tools with the old mind-set.

## APPLYING YOUR KNOWLEDGE

Complete some or all of the following activities throughout the month to apply this concept to your personal and professional lives.

- Refer to the "Reviewing the Underlying Principles" exercise on page 161. If you answered "sometimes" or "rarely" to any of the categories, why? What is causing the gap between stated values and behavior? What can you do to influence and improve this situation? Work on addressing this situation over the coming month.

________________________________________

________________________________________

________________________________________

________________________________________

________________________________________

________________________________________

________________________________________

________________________________________

________________________________________

- Refer to the "Focusing on Family Results" exercise on page 166. Over the coming month, try using a new reward system and see how it influences behavior. Record your results in your journal at the back of this workbook.

- Refer to your conclusions in the "Reflecting on Your Team's Current Alignment" exercise. What steps can you take over the next month to correct any misalignments you identified? Record your results in your journal at the back of this workbook.

______________________________________________

______________________________________________

______________________________________________

______________________________________________

______________________________________________

______________________________________________

- Read *Teaching the Elephant to Dance: the Manager's Guide to Empowering Change* by J.A. Belasco.

- Teach the main ideas of this chapter to at least two other people. List their names.

______________________________________________

______________________________________________

- Report your results to friends, colleagues and family members. List their names.

______________________________________________

______________________________________________

*Chapter* 13

# THE EMPOWERING VOICE—RELEASING PASSION AND TALENT

*Before you begin this section of the workbook, read pages 249–268 in* The 8th Habit, *review the underlying principles listed here or read the summary in the Appendix.*

> *The best way to inspire people to a superior performance is to convince them by everything you do and by your everyday attitude that you are wholeheartedly supporting them.*
>
> —HAROLD S. GENEEN, FORMER CHAIRMAN OF ITT

## REVIEWING THE UNDERLYING PRINCIPLES

- *Empowering is the fruit* of the other three leadership roles (modeling, pathfinding and aligning). It is the result of personal and group trustworthiness. When you inspire trust (modeling), create vision (pathfinding) and align results (aligning), you can begin to tap into the passion, energy and drive of your department, team or family—in other words, you and they will find your voices and become empowered.
- Tapping into this voice (empowerment) is vitally important in the Information/Knowledge Worker Age because wealth creation has shifted from products to people. People are a team's most important asset. *Knowledge workers have choices* and will migrate to those teams, departments or organizations that provide the best choices—where they feel empowered and their voices are heard.

- The *top three reasons* empowerment is stifled are:
  - Manager is afraid to let go.
  - Systems are misaligned. (Sound familiar?)
  - Manager lacks skills.
- However, if you have mastered modeling, pathfinding and aligning you have overcome these obstacles and are perfectly positioned to empower your employees.
- *Directed autonomy* is when you no longer control people, but enable them—you co-mission, remove barriers and become a source of help and support.
- Successful empowerment rests in a commitment to work with team members using *Win-Win Agreements.* In a department or team, this means the four needs of the organization (financial health, growth, synergistic relationships and meaningful contribution) overlap with the four needs of the individual (to live—economic, to learn—mental, to love—social emotional, and to leave a legacy—spiritual).
- You are probably wondering, what about accountability? This system can actually *increase accountability* because empowered employees are accountable for themselves. (After all, who is in a better position to know the score?) Evidence shows that people (especially those provided with peer feedback) are much tougher on themselves than a boss would be. Think how absurd it would be to work to empower and build trust with your employees and then say, "But I can't trust you to be honest about your work—I still know best." It would be a perfect example of misalignment of values and results.
- In this environment, the boss's role is to act as a *servant-leader* who assists by asking questions such as:
  - How is it going?
  - What are you learning?
  - What are your goals?
  - How can I help you?
  - How am I doing as a helper?

- When this system is in place, trust as a verb and a noun is fully established. Trust is shared and reciprocated.
- You may be thinking, "That's a lovely idea, but it doesn't apply to the jobs in my team. I don't need empowered workers; I just need people to do the simple tasks I tell them to do." However, *any job can be a knowledge worker* job if you allow it to be by applying the whole-person model.

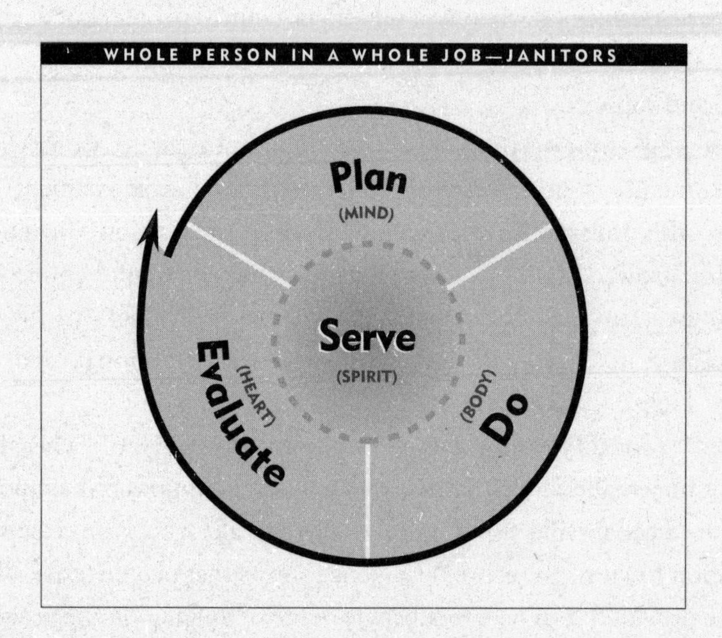


- By empowering people even at the lowest levels (recall both the janitor story on pages 262–264 and the Grameen bank story on pages 6–9 in *The 8th Habit*), you *tap into their highest potential*, and both you and they reap the benefits of their creativity.
- Only 45 percent of xQ respondents say they feel their contributions at work are recognized and appreciated. Empowering the remaining 55 percent would allow your team to *harness the creativity and spirit of 100 percent of your people.*

## LEARNING OBJECTIVES

If you study and apply the underlying principles in this chapter for a month, you can expect to:

- Learn how empowering employees increases accountability.
- Understand how to act as a servant-leader.
- Implement the whole-person model that makes every job a knowledge worker job.
- Analyze your results to find out if you are unintentionally enabling irresponsibility and make plans to correct this issue.

## ANALYZING AN EFFECTIVE WIN-WIN SITUATION

Win-Win Agreements are an effective way to clarify expectations, change your thinking to mutual benefit and build commitment around desired results.

Think about something you've done—a project or job—that went smoothly and for which you got great results. Why did you have confidence in that area?

______________________________________________

______________________________________________

______________________________________________

______________________________________________

______________________________________________

______________________________________________

For the project or job you identified here, list what the win-win elements would have looked like had you created a formal agreement.

Desired Results: ______________________________

______________________________

______________________________

Guidelines: ______________________________

______________________________

______________________________

Resources: ______________________________

______________________________

______________________________

Accountability: ______________________________

______________________________

______________________________

Consequences: ______________________________

______________________________

______________________________

## USING THE WHOLE-PERSON MODEL

Reread "The Case of the Janitors" on pages 262–264 in *The 8th Habit*. Then circle the statement that most closely describes the way you lead.

1. When handing off work:
    a. I tell people exactly what to do, step by step, and how to do it.
    b. I am specific about what needs to be done and offer guidelines as to how to do it.
    c. I share the vision of what needs to happen. I make myself available, but let others decide how to do it.
2. When other people need help:
    a. I find out what the problem is and tell them exactly how to solve it.
    b. I find out what is needed and give guidance and help.
    c. I find out what is needed and offer suggestions when they ask for my expertise.
3. When things go wrong:
    a. I fix the problem—that's what I'm paid for.
    b. I give directions as to what people can do to fix the problem and help fix it with them.
    c. I ask for suggestions and provide recommendations as needed.
4. When presenting our work to others:
    a. I represent the team.
    b. I work closely with the team to determine who should report what and how.
    c. I let those doing the work make the presentation.
5. When decisions need to be made:
    a. They must go through me.
    b. I work to help my people make more of their own decisions.
    c. People make decisions within specific guidelines, but check with me beyond those guidelines.

6. When it comes to those I lead:
   a. Not much seems to get done when I am away.
   b. I work closely with them to determine who is doing what by when.
   c. I know the things they are working on, although I don't get involved much in the details of what they do.

How closely does your management style reflect the Whole-Person Model? Why?

______________________________________________________________

______________________________________________________________

______________________________________________________________

______________________________________________________________

______________________________________________________________

How might your style affect the people you work with?

______________________________________________________________

______________________________________________________________

______________________________________________________________

______________________________________________________________

______________________________________________________________

Now, retake the survey with your family in mind.

Does your work management style match your home management style? If not, why?

## VIEWING THE FILM *The Nature of Leadership*

As you view the film *The Nature of Leadership* on your companion DVD or online, personally reflect on the underlying principles of this leadership framework.

How will you internalize and act on these principles as challenged in the film?

## UNDERSTANDING THE EFFECTS OF MALICIOUS OBEDIENCE

What would happen if you *only* followed the exact rules for your job and did nothing outside the rules?

___

___

___

___

___

___

___

What would happen if your teammates did the same?

___

___

___

___

___

___

What does your answer say about your job and, more important, about your level of involvement? Do you work outside the rules? Why?

## APPLYING YOUR KNOWLEDGE

Complete some or all of the following activities throughout the month to apply this concept to your personal and professional lives.

- Recall the story of the mom who unintentionally enabled her children's irresponsibility (pages 250–252 in *The 8th Habit*).

Take a hard look at any dysfunctional results you see in your family. Are you unintentionally enabling irresponsibility? How?

What do you need to do to strengthen your relationship with your family?

______________________________________________

______________________________________________

______________________________________________

______________________________________________

______________________________________________

______________________________________________

What can you do to better communicate to your children their worth and potential?

______________________________________________

______________________________________________

______________________________________________

______________________________________________

______________________________________________

______________________________________________

What do you plan to do to increase the trust in your relationships?

______________________________________________

What training do you need to provide to help them?

List the results you would like to see here. (Note: You may also want to refer to the "Focusing on Family Results" exercise on page 166 in this workbook.)

What behaviors do *you* need to change to address this situation? (Remember, you can only control yourself, not others. You need to encourage the results you want.)

______________________________________________

______________________________________________

______________________________________________

______________________________________________

______________________________________________

- Over the next month, implement a plan to change *your* behavior and to put in place a new Win-Win Agreement with your family. You can use the following form and example as a guide.

| **Win-Win Agreement** | |
|---|---|
| **Desired Results:** What's the end in mind? What are the outcomes we want? | |
| **Guidelines:** What rules do we follow? What are the guidelines for accomplishing the results? | |
| **Resources:** What resources do we have to work with (e.g., people, money, tools, materials, technology)? | |
| **Accountability:** How will we measure how well it's going? | |
| **Consequences:** What are the rewards of achieving the outcome? What are the consequences of not achieving the outcome? | |

For example, the Win-Win Agreement from the story on pages 250–252 in *The 8th Habit* could have looked like this:

| **Win-Win Agreement** | |
|---|---|
| **Desired Results:** What's the end in mind? What are the outcomes we want? | Children responsible for themselves; mom less stressed; mornings more pleasant for everyone |
| **Guidelines:** What rules do we follow? What are the guidelines for accomplishing the results? | Children getting up when their alarms go off; mom and dad not nagging |
| **Resources:** What resources do we have to work with (e.g., people, money, tools, materials, technology)? | Mom and dad, washing machine, alarm clocks |
| **Accountability:** How will we measure how well it's going? | Downstairs by 6:45 a.m.; meeting occasionally to check progress |
| **Consequences:** What are the rewards of achieving the outcome? What are the consequences of not achieving the outcome? | Earlier bed time for being late; pleasant mornings |

- Recall your answers to the "Using the Whole-Person Model" exercise. List those questions to which you chose answer a.

______________________________________________

______________________________________________

Why did you choose that answer?

______________________________________________

______________________________________________

______________________________________________

Would it be possible to implement a Whole-Person Model instead?

________________________________________

________________________________________

________________________________________

If not, why? What are the obstacles?

________________________________________

________________________________________

________________________________________

What could you do to remove these obstacles?

________________________________________

________________________________________

________________________________________

Most teams and departments are overmanaged and underled. If you are finding it difficult to give up control, you may be stuck in the manager mind-set. You will not be able to build trust and empower others until you move beyond this obstacle.

- Over the next month, work on taking the servant-leader role by asking questions such as those shown in the diagram below. Record your results in your journal at the back of this workbook. You may want to post a copy of these questions on your wall to remind yourself of the behaviors to strive for in the servant-leader role.

**SERVANT LEADER**

*(Mutual Accountability)*

1. **How is it going?** (Scoreboard, data)
2. **What are you learning?**
3. **What are your goals?**
4. **How can I help you?**
5. **How am I doing as a helper?**

- Evaluate your team and family for opportunities to implement the Whole-Person Model (see page 264 in *The 8th Habit*). Are there relationships or job functions you supervise that could benefit from empowerment? Record your results in your journal at the back of this workbook.

- Read *Now Discover Your Strengths* by Marcus Buckingham and Donald O. Clifton.

- Read *Leadership Is an Art* by Max De Pree.

- Teach the main ideas of this chapter to at least two other people. List their names.

________________________________________

________________________________________

________________________________________

- Report your results to friends, colleagues and family members. List their names.

_______________

_______________

_______________

_______________

_______________

*Chapter* 14

# THE 8TH HABIT AND THE SWEET SPOT

*Before you begin this section of the workbook, read pages 270–291 in* The 8th Habit, *review the underlying principles listed here or read the summary in the Appendix.*

> *The difference between what we are doing and what we're capable of doing would solve most of the world's problems.*
> *—Mahatma Gandhi*

## REVIEWING THE UNDERLYING PRINCIPLES

- To help other people find their voices, successful leaders practice the 4 Roles of Leadership in this way:
  - Modeling: Inspires trust without expecting it (personal moral authority).
  - Pathfinding: Creates order without demanding it (visionary moral authority).
  - Aligning: Nourishes both vision and empowerment without proclaiming them (institutional moral authority).
  - Empowering: Unleashes the human potential without externally motivating it (cultural moral authority).
- The 4 Roles of Leadership can be boiled down to two words: *focus* and *execution*. Focus includes modeling and pathfinding. Execution includes aligning and empowering.

- *Execution* (or aligning and empowering) is the great unaddressed issue in most organizations today, including families. There are six core drivers of execution in an organization. Think about these drivers for all roles of your life:
  - *Clarity:* People know the goals and priorities.
  - *Commitment:* People are involved in setting the goals and priorities and are therefore committed to them.
  - *Translation:* People know what they are supposed to do as individuals to help meet the goals.
  - *Enabling:* People have the structure, systems and empowerment to do the job well.
  - *Synergy:* People work well together to create Third Alternatives.
  - *Accountability:* People are accountable for the results.
- The three levels of greatness are: *personal* greatness, *leadership* greatness, and *organizational* greatness, as depicted here.

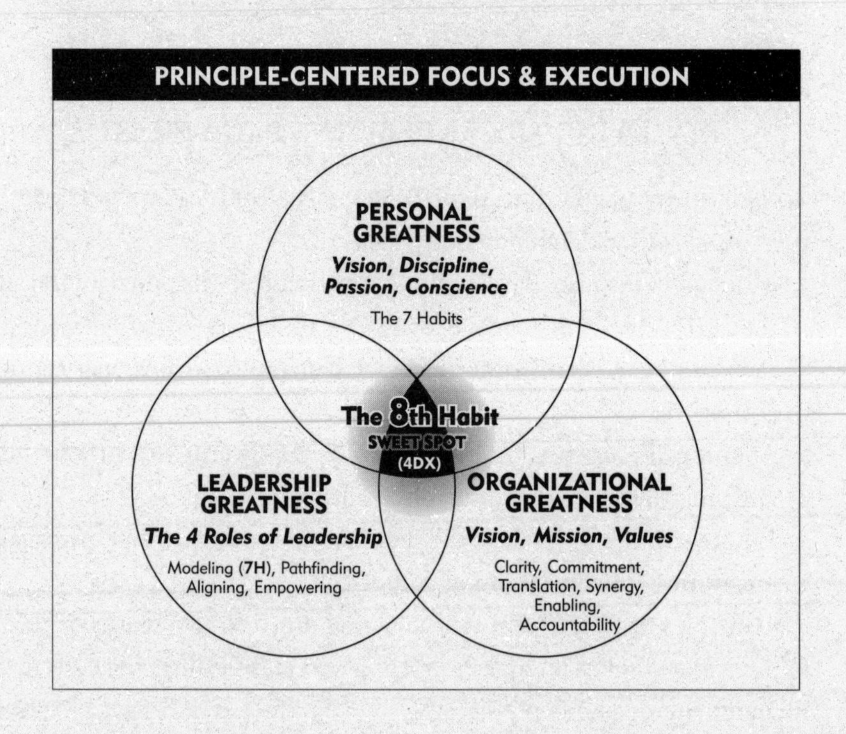

- The 8th Habit sweet spot is the overlapping of the three levels of greatness that results in the 4 Disciplines of Execution. Applying the four disciplines can close execution gaps and improve a family's, team's or department's ability to reach their goals. The four disciplines are:
  - *Discipline 1:* Focus on the wildly important (only a few goals at a time).
  - *Discipline 2:* Create a compelling scoreboard (a way to list and track progress of the goals).
  - *Discipline 3:* Translate lofty goals into specific actions (create prioritized task lists to reach the goal).
  - *Discipline 4:* Hold each other accountable all of the time (follow up on progress, provide incentive and reward or correct appropriately).

## LEARNING OBJECTIVES

If you study and apply the underlying principles in this chapter for a month, you can expect to:

- Understand how personal greatness, leadership greatness and organizational greatness combine to create the 8th Habit sweet spot.
- Provide focus to your team, department or family by creating a scoreboard for the high-priority goals.
- Practice better execution by assessing and then improving one or more of the six drivers of execution and by translating the high-priority goals into specific actions for you and the people you lead.
- Focus on important triage issues by conducting an accountability session.
- Feel the thrill of hitting the 8th Habit sweet spot as you and the people you lead actually go to work to achieve greatness.

## EXAMINING THE SIX CORE DRIVERS IN ACTION

Choose two of the six core drivers below and describe a specific time in your company, team or family when that driver was executed well or not executed well.

*Clarity:* People know the goals and priorities.

______________________________________________

______________________________________________

______________________________________________

______________________________________________

*Commitment:* People are involved in setting the goals and priorities and are therefore committed to them.

______________________________________________

______________________________________________

______________________________________________

______________________________________________

*Translation:* People know what they are supposed to do as individuals to help meet the goals.

______________________________________________

______________________________________________

______________________________________________

______________________________________________

*Enabling:* People have the structure, systems and empowerment to do the job well.

______________________________

______________________________

______________________________

*Synergy:* People work well together to create Third Alternatives.

______________________________

______________________________

______________________________

*Accountability:* People are accountable for the results.

______________________________

______________________________

______________________________

What reasons contributed to those core drivers being executed or not executed well?

______________________________

______________________________

## REFLECTING ON THE SWEET SPOT

In tennis or golf, the sweet spot is the place on the racquet or club that connects perfectly with the ball. When you connect with it, you know you've hit it—it resonates and feels just right. With no more effort than usual, that connection with the center releases a burst of power, and the ball is sent soaring much farther and faster than usual.

In *The 8th Habit*, the sweet spot is another way of referring to the power that is released when you find your voice as an individual and as a team. Describe a time when you served on a team that hit the sweet spot, when personal greatness, leadership greatness and organizational greatness all came together.

What results were you able to accomplish on that team that were out of the ordinary?

Describe your personal feelings about serving on that team. What was particularly gratifying?

## DISCOVERING THE 4 DISCIPLINES OF EXECUTION

The 4 Disciplines of Execution are the result of the sweet spot when the three kinds of greatness (personal, interpersonal and organizational) come together.

### Discipline 1—Focus on the Wildly Important

A wildly important goal carries serious consequences. Failure to achieve this goal renders all other achievements relatively inconsequential.

The Importance Screen is a tool to help analyze which goals are wildly important and will best help us execute our strategic plan. Use this tool to prioritize goals by running them through the economic, strategic and stakeholder screens.

Instructions:

1. List your team's or department's potential goals on the table on the next page in the Potential Goals column. (You could also do this for your family if you slightly modify the criteria of each screen.)
2. For each screen (economic, strategic and stakeholder), rate each goal on a scale of – 1 to 4, where 4 = high positive impact, 0 = no impact, and – 1 = negative impact. Consider the criteria of each screen before rating the goals.

| Economic Screen | Strategic Screen | Stakeholder Screen |
|---|---|---|
| Scale –1 to 4<br>Consider these economic criteria:<br>• Grows revenue<br>• Reduces costs<br>• Improves cash flow<br>• Improves profitability<br>• Other economic criteria | Scale –1 to 4<br>Consider these strategic criteria:<br>• Directly supports the team goals<br>• Leverages core competencies<br>• Increases market strength<br>• Increases competitive advantage<br>• Other strategic criteria | Scale –1 to 4<br>Consider these stakeholder criteria:<br>• Increases customer loyalty<br>• Ignites passion and energy of our people<br>• Favorably impacts suppliers/vendors, partners, investors<br>• Other stakeholder criteria |

3. Total the score for each goal in the Total column.
4. Do a gut check. Are you facing the brutal realities?
5. Using the score totals and the gut check, place a check mark by the two or three goals that are truly most important.

| **Potential Goals** | **Economic (−1 to 4)** | **Strategic (−1 to 4)** | **Stakeholder (−1 to 4)** | **Total:** | ✓ |
|---|---|---|---|---|---|
| 1. | | | | | |
| 2. | | | | | |
| 3. | | | | | |
| 4. | | | | | |
| 5. | | | | | |
| 6. | | | | | |
| 7. | | | | | |

**VIEWING THE FILM *It's Not Just Important, It's Wildly Important***

After you view the film *It's Not Just Important, It's Wildly Important* on your companion DVD or online, answer the following question.

Did you relate to any of the execution problems presented? What did you recognize in your own department or team in this film?

---

---

---

---

---

---

---

---

---

---

---

**Discipline 2—Create a Compelling Scoreboard**

A scoreboard allows you to leverage a basic principle: People play differently when they're keeping score. Having a compelling, visible, accessible scoreboard for your strategic plan and goals allows work groups to measure their success and monitor how they are doing on their key priorities.

Identify the key measures for your team goals and make a visual representation of them. Ensure that the scoreboard clarifies three things: the current result, the target result and the deadline.

List your top priorities or wildly important goals. (Your wildly important goals are the ones you placed a check mark by in the preceding table.)

________________________________________

________________________________________

________________________________________

________________________________________

For each wildly important goal you listed, write down the following information (you may have to make your best guess at the current results if the goal is not something you have measured in the past):

| **Wildly Important Goal** | **Current Result (where we are now)** | **Target Result (where we need to be)** | **Deadline (by when)** |
|---|---|---|---|
| 1. | | | |
| 2. | | | |
| 3. | | | |

**Discipline 3—Translate Lofty Goals Into Specific Actions**

Coming up with a new goal or strategy is one thing, but actually turning that goal into action, new behaviors and activities at all levels is another. Goals will never be achieved until everyone on the team knows exactly what they're supposed to do about them.

To practice this discipline, your team must identify new and better behaviors needed to achieve their goals, then translate them into weekly and daily tasks. Practice how you would implement this discipline below.

| Goal | New Behavior | Associated Weekly or Daily Task |
|---|---|---|
| Example: Reduce dollars spent on last-minute copying at the all-night copy center, which is 33 percent more expensive than our corporate copy center. | Use a personal planner to manage projects, priorities and time. | Refer to a personal planner each morning to anticipate when copying deadlines are approaching.<br>Coordinate team members' available time at weekly staff meeting. Ask for help if needed. |
| | | |
| | | |
| | | |
| | | |
| | | |

**Discipline 4—Hold Each Other Accountable All of the Time**

In the most effective teams, people meet frequently (monthly, weekly or daily) to account for their commitments, examine the scoreboard, resolve issues and decide how to support one another. Unless everyone on a team holds everyone else accountable (all of the time), the process will fail.

These accountability sessions are not like typical staff meetings where many topics are discussed, some of which are irrelevant and merely keep people away from their desks and their real work. An accountability session's purpose is to move the key goals forward.

The three key practices to include in an accountability session are:

- *Triage reporting*—As in a hospital where patients are treated in order of seriousness, not arrival, so, too, an accountability session focuses on the vital few issues. In triage reporting, everyone reports quickly on the vital few issues, leaving the less important issues for another time. Focus on key results, major problems, and high-level issues.
- *Finding Third Alternatives*—Effective accountability sessions drive team members to focus intensely on achieving key goals. A new goal the team has never achieved requires doing things the team has never done. The team may need to look for a Third Alternative or another course of action.
- *Clearing the path*—Effective leadership clears the path of barriers and aligns goals and systems so that others can achieve their goals. In true win-win fashion, the manager agrees to do things only he or she can do to enable the worker to achieve the goal. Team members can also clear the path for other team members. They may ask each other, "How can I clear the path for you?" or "What can we do for you to help you get that done?"

Accountability sessions are not like staff meetings, so the behaviors exhibited in the two meetings must also be different. List below the behaviors you must foster to convert your typical staff meeting into an accountability session.

| Current Staff Meeting Behavior | Desired Accountability Session Behavior |
|---|---|
| **Triage reporting** | |
| Example: Death march around the room where people feel pressure to talk while everyone else checks out | Quick reporting of vital few issues |
| | |
| | |
| | |
| **Finding Third Alternatives** | |
| Example: Wisdom of the lone genius | Wisdom of the group |
| | |
| | |
| | |
| **Clearing the path** | |
| Example: You're on your own | We're in this together |
| | |
| | |
| | |

## APPLYING YOUR KNOWLEDGE

Complete some or all of the following activities throughout the month to apply this concept to your personal and professional lives.

- View the film *Max & Max* again on your companion DVD or online, then read Appendix 7 in *The 8th Habit* on pages 374–378. Choose a situation in which you are either acting as Max or Mr. Harold. In what ways could you apply ethos, pathos and logos or the 4 roles to trim-tab your way out of the situation? Record your thoughts in the journal at the back of this workbook.

- Write down one way you could improve the execution of the group you lead in each of the six areas below. For example, in the area of clarity, if you are a manager make sure your employees understand the high-priority goals. In the area of translation, if you are a mother make sure your children know what they are suppose to do to help the family reach its goals. Then make plans this month to work on those areas you selected.

*Clarity:* People know the goals and priorities.

________________________________________

________________________________________

________________________________________

*Commitment:* People are involved in setting the goals and priorities and are therefore committed to them.

________________________________________

________________________________________

________________________________________

*Translation:* People know what they are supposed to do as individuals to meet the goals.

______________________________________________

______________________________________________

______________________________________________

*Enabling:* People have the structure, systems and empowerment to do the job well.

______________________________________________

______________________________________________

______________________________________________

*Synergy:* People work well together to create Third Alternatives.

______________________________________________

______________________________________________

______________________________________________

*Accountability:* People are accountable for the results.

______________________________________________

______________________________________________

______________________________________________

- Discuss the information from the exercise "Discipline 2—Create a Compelling Scoreboard" on page 198 with your team or department. With a small, cross-sectional group of people, convert the information into a visual representation for your team. Some examples of scoreboards include a bar graph, trend line, pie chart, Gantt chart, thermometer, speedometer or scale. Make sure it is visible, dynamic and accessible. Consider including measures in the scoreboard regarding principle-centered values.

- Work with your team or department to translate the lofty goals on the scoreboard into specific actions and behaviors for you and the people you lead.

- Hold a family meeting to create a family scoreboard. Allow all members to have a say in what the most important family goals are, where the family is currently, where the family would like to be and what the deadlines will be for each goal. Discuss ways to hold each other accountable for achieving the family goals.

- Conduct an accountability session this month with your team or department. Use the three practices of triage reporting, finding Third Alternatives, and clearing the path.

- Take the online personal xQ survey to assess your individual team's ability to focus and execute on top priorities. Go to www.The8thHabit.com/offers for directions as to how to take the survey.

- Teach the main ideas of this chapter to at least two other people. List their names.

________________________________________

________________________________________

________________________________________

- Report your results to friends, colleagues and family members. List their names.

______________________________________________________________

______________________________________________________________

______________________________________________________________

______________________________________________________________

______________________________________________________________

*Chapter* 15

# USING OUR VOICES WISELY TO SERVE OTHERS

*Before you begin this section of the workbook, read pages 292–317 in* The 8th Habit, *review the underlying principles listed here or read the summary in the Appendix.*

> *You have not done enough, you have never done enough so long as it is still possible that you have something of value to contribute.*
>
> —DAG HAMMARSKJÖLD

## REVIEWING THE UNDERLYING PRINCIPLES

- Why do we want to find our voice? Why do we want to help others find theirs? The 8th Habit is fueled by one great overarching purpose: to serve human needs.
- Organizations of all types (companies, educational institutions, governments, nonprofit organizations, families) are established to serve human needs. There is no other reason for their existence.
- What will be the next age in history after the Information/Knowledge Worker Age? The Age of Wisdom. Wisdom can only come in time after humility and courage create integrity.

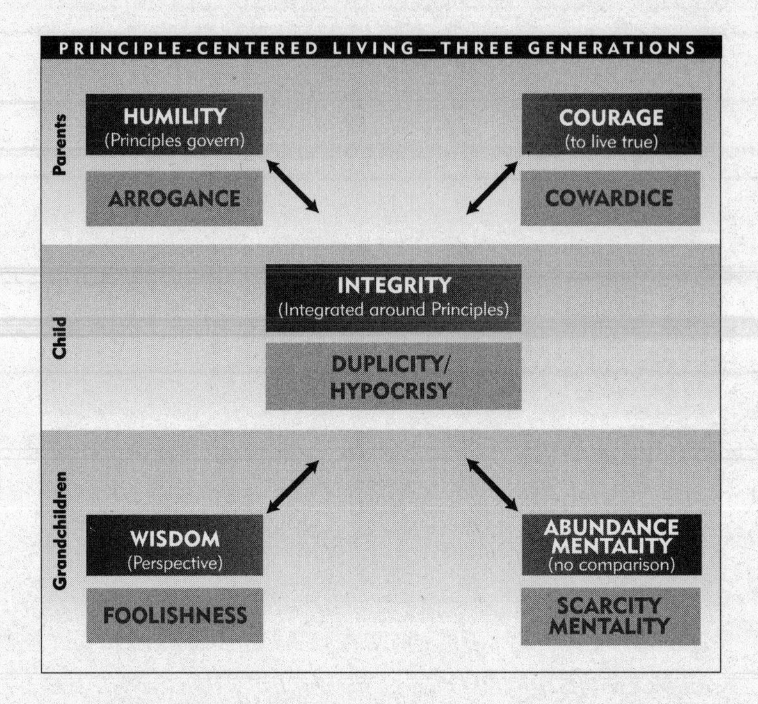


- Wisdom teaches the notion of servant-leadership—service above self. History is full of examples of servant-leaders, all of whom had moral authority (character strength). Most of them also achieved formal authority (position, title, etc.) through their dedication to serving others. This kind of heartfelt service is the essence of moral authority.
- Moral authority is like an ecosystem. It begins with individual *visionary* moral authority. A leader with moral authority can imbed principles in the fiber of an institution to create *institutionalized* moral authority. Then, gradually, a civic society can develop its own *cultural* moral authority. Remember the words of Emile Durkheim: "When mores [culture and customs] are sufficient, laws are unnecessary. When mores are insufficient, laws are unenforceable." Sufficient cultural mores are a reflection of a society with cultural moral authority.
- *The 8th Habit* teaches one central paradigm: that people are *whole* people—body, mind, heart and spirit.

## LEARNING OBJECTIVES

If you study and apply the underlying principles in this chapter for a month, you can expect to:

- Understand how moral authority promotes servant-leadership.
- Recognize that leadership and servant-leadership is a choice, not necessarily a position.
- Determine if you are leading using moral authority or simply your position for each of your leadership roles.
- Identify things you can do to become a better servant-leader.
- Learn to use wisdom instead of cultural overlay to solve problems.
- Select an area of focus for the body, mind, heart and spirit that relates to the four intelligences, the four attributes and the 4 Roles of Leadership.

## EXAMINING HOW ORGANIZATIONS ARE ESTABLISHED TO SERVE HUMAN NEEDS

Read the following, from *The 8th Habit*:

> Business has become the most powerful institution on the planet. The dominant institution in any society needs to take responsibility for the whole. But business has not had such a tradition. This is a new role, not well understood or accepted. Built on the concept of capitalism and free enterprise from the beginning was the assumption that the actions of many units of individual enterprise, responding to market forces and guided by the "invisible hand" of Adam Smith, would somehow add up to desirable outcomes. But in the last decade of the 20th century, it has become clear that the "invisible hand" is faltering. It depended on overarching meanings and values that are no longer present. So business has to adapt to a tradition it has never had throughout the entire history of capitalism: to share the responsibility of the whole. Every decision that is

> made, every action that is taken, must be viewed in light of that responsibility.
>
> —*Willis Harmon, cofounder of the World Business Academy*

Is this statement true? Why or why not?

"Every decision that is made, every action that is taken, must be viewed in light of that responsibility." What can organizations do to ensure that this happens?

## CHOOSING TO LEAD

Review Table 10 on page 303 in *The 8th Habit.* Think about your leadership roles, and then answer the questions below.

Can you think of a time when you exerted your influence primarily using your position power rather than using moral authority and persuasion? Describe the example. What were the short- and long-term results?

______________________________________________

______________________________________________

______________________________________________

______________________________________________

______________________________________________

______________________________________________

______________________________________________

______________________________________________

Can you think of a time when you exerted your influence through moral authority rather than position? Describe the situation. What were the short- and long-term results?

______________________________________________

______________________________________________

______________________________________________

For those times when you used your power to lead, what areas on Table 10 on page 303 could you improve in? Think honestly and deeply about each statement on the table.

## BECOMING A SERVANT-LEADER

Think of a leader (formal or informal) in your life who adopted the attitude of servant-leader—one who served, supported and contributed.

What attitudes or actions first let you know that he or she was a servant-leader?

____________________________________________________________

____________________________________________________________

____________________________________________________________

____________________________________________________________

What was your reaction to this leadership style? What were your initial thoughts or feelings?

____________________________________________________________

____________________________________________________________

____________________________________________________________

____________________________________________________________

How did this management style affect your actions?

____________________________________________________________

____________________________________________________________

____________________________________________________________

What results were attained that might not have been possible without this servant-leader model?

______________________________________________________________________

______________________________________________________________________

______________________________________________________________________

How can you become a servant-leader? What attitudes or actions will you have to change?

______________________________________________________________________

______________________________________________________________________

______________________________________________________________________

## VIEWING THE FILM *Gandhi*

As you view this scene from the film *Gandhi*, you'll observe a person of weakness and pride, but also a person who used his birth-gifts to develop humility, courage, integrity, discipline and vision. He is a beautiful example of a person who developed moral authority, and the world is different because of him. (Note: This film is available only on the companion DVD.)

As you view the film *Gandhi* on your companion DVD, study the nuances of:

- Words and facial expressions.
- Initiatives and reactions.
- Development of mores, norms, values, goals and vision.

What did Gandhi say or do that demonstrated he was a servant-leader?

________________________________________________

________________________________________________

________________________________________________

________________________________________________

Are there some tasks in your work that are analogous to "raking and covering the latrine?"

________________________________________________

________________________________________________

________________________________________________

________________________________________________

What is your attitude toward these tasks? Do you sometimes feel these tasks are for other people to do, but not for you?

________________________________________________

________________________________________________

________________________________________________

________________________________________________

## USING WISDOM TO SOLVE PROBLEMS

In the space below, write three examples of common personal, relationship and organizational desired results. Think about the flawed cultural overlay that creates a dilemma in achieving the desired results. Then reason out what wisdom would dictate. Several examples are given to get you started.

| Desired Results | Flawed Cultural Overlay | What would wisdom say to do? |
|---|---|---|
| **Personal Level** | | |
| Example: People want peace of mind and good relationships. | People want to keep their habits and lifestyle. | The person would need to win a private victory by sacrificing what "I want" for a higher, more important purpose and for what is right. |
| | | |
| | | |
| | | |
| **Relationship Level** | | |
| Example: People want relationships of trust. | Individuals think more in terms of "me" (my wants, needs and rights). | Focus on trust-building principles and sacrificing "me" for "we." |
| | | |
| | | |
| | | |

| Desired Results | Flawed Cultural Overlay | What would wisdom say to do? |
|---|---|---|
| **Organizational Level** | | |
| Example: Management wants more for less. | Employees want more of what's in it for them for less time and effort. | Develop a Third Alternative, Win-Win Agreement through sacrificing control or abdication for empowerment, so that management and employees are on the same page of unleashing human potential and producing more for less. |
| | | |
| | | |
| | | |

## APPLYING YOUR KNOWLEDGE

Complete some or all of the following activities throughout the month to apply this concept to your personal and professional lives.

- Review "Level 5 Leadership," Figure 15.4 on page 300 in *The 8th Habit*. Consider leaders you know who fall into each of those categories. In your journal at the back of this workbook, outline specific areas in which you could improve to become a level 5 leader. Apply your ideas during the month.

- Refer to Figure 15.7 on page 312 in *The 8th Habit*. For each row (body, mind, heart and spirit), select one column to work on. For example, you may choose to work on modeling for the body, practicing self-discipline for the mind, increasing your emotional intelligence for the heart and empowering others for the spirit. Write your area of focus below, then go to work.

*Body* (to live):_______________________________________________

_______________________________________________________________

_______________________________________________________________

*Mind* (to learn):______________________________________________

_______________________________________________________________

_______________________________________________________________

*Heart* (to love):______________________________________________

_______________________________________________________________

_______________________________________________________________

*Spirit* (to leave a legacy):____________________________________

_______________________________________________________________

_______________________________________________________________

- Consider what Winston Churchill said: "To every man there comes in his lifetime that special moment when he is figuratively tapped on the shoulder and offered a chance to do a very special thing, unique to him and fitted to his talents. What a tragedy if that moment finds him unprepared or unqualified for the work which would be his finest hour." What is your conscience telling you right now when you read that quote? What opportunities are present at this moment that could represent your finest hour if you will have the courage to take it? Record your thoughts in the journal at the end of this workbook.

- Teach the main ideas of this chapter to at least two other people. List their names.

________________________________________________

________________________________________________

________________________________________________

________________________________________________

- Report your results to friends, colleagues and family members. List their names.

________________________________________________

________________________________________________

________________________________________________

________________________________________________

________________________________________________

________________________________________________

## TYING IT ALL TOGETHER—FINDING YOUR VOICE

To be successful in the Information/Knowledge Worker Age requires different habits than before—different skills, knowledge and attitudes. The 8th Habit: Find Your Voice and Help Others to Find Theirs is a process for moving from effectiveness to greatness.

Find your voice by:

- Recognizing and using your power of choice.
- Aligning your personal values with principles or natural laws to develop moral authority.
- Tapping into your four intelligences.

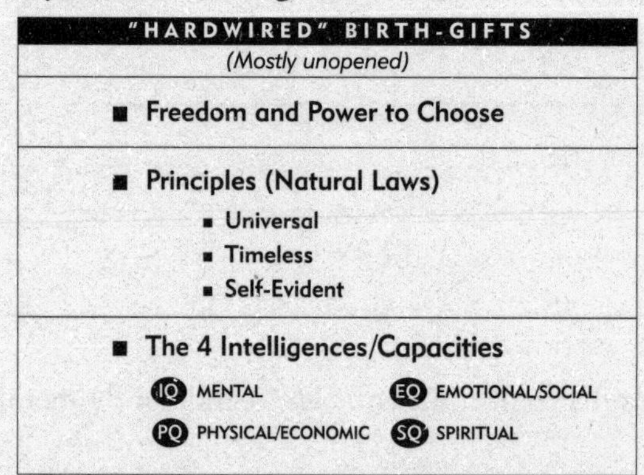


- Finding and expressing your voice means to live as a whole person.

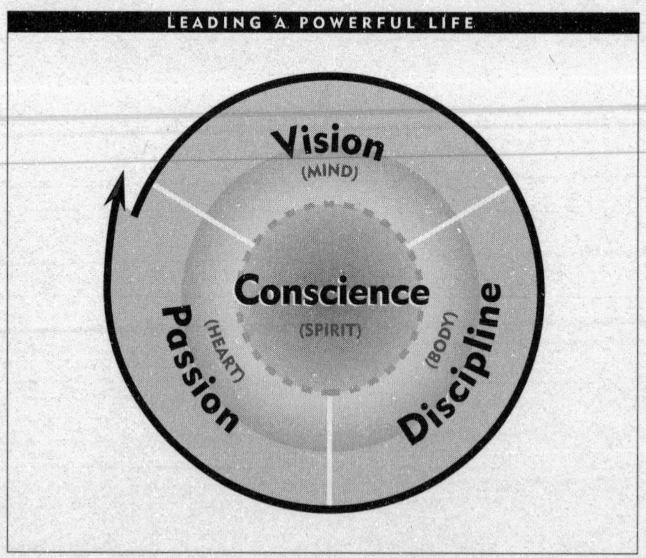

## TYING IT ALL TOGETHER—
## HELPING OTHERS TO FIND THEIR VOICE

Helping others find their voices requires that you practice the 4 Roles of Leadership:

- Pathfinding
- Aligning
- Empowering
- Modeling

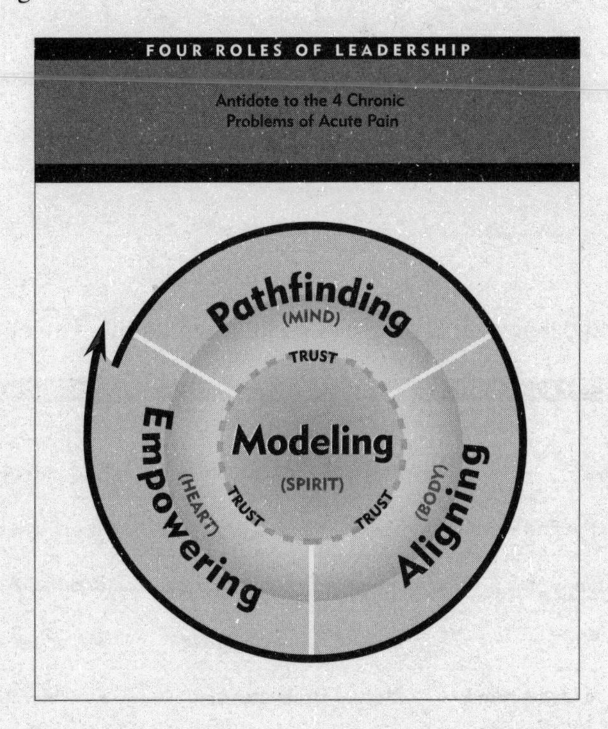

Empower others by treating them as whole people in a whole job.

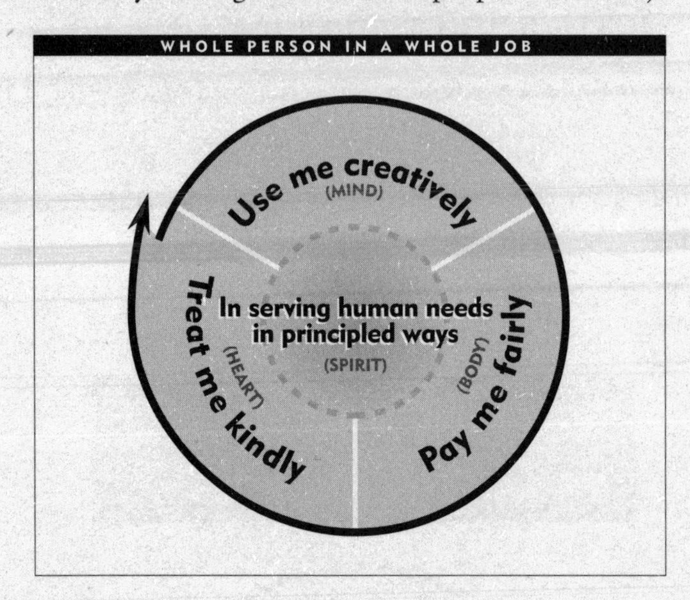


Model desired behavior by living the 7 Habits of Highly Effective People.

**PRINCIPLES AND PARADIGMS EMBODIED IN THE 7 HABITS**

| *Habit* | *Principle* | *Paradigm* |
|---|---|---|
| ❶ Be Proactive | Responsibility/Initiative | Self-determination |
| ❷ Begin with the End in Mind | Vision/Values | Two Creations / Focus |
| ❸ Put First Things First | Integrity/Execution | Priority / Action |
| ❹ Think Win-Win | Mutual Respect/Benefit | Abundance |
| ❺ Seek First to Understand, Then to be Understood | Mutual Understanding | Consideration Courage |
| ❻ Synergize | Creative Cooperation | Value Differences |
| ❼ Sharpen the Saw | Renewal | Whole Person |

Work within your Circle of Influence and use ethos, pathos and logos to become a trim-tab—a model for positive change.

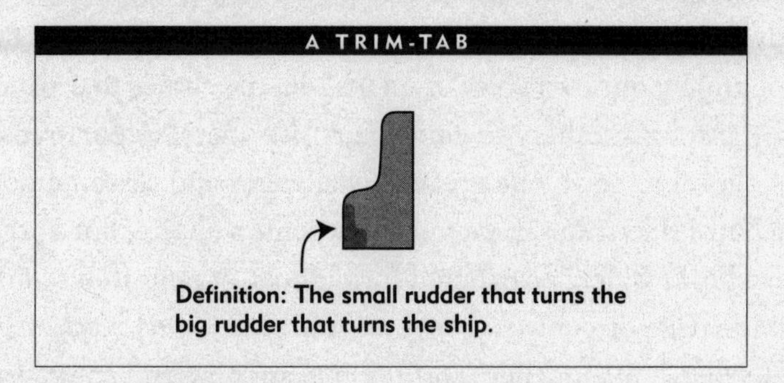


Find the sweet spot through principle-centered focus and execution in:

- Personal greatness
- Leadership greatness
- Organizational greatness

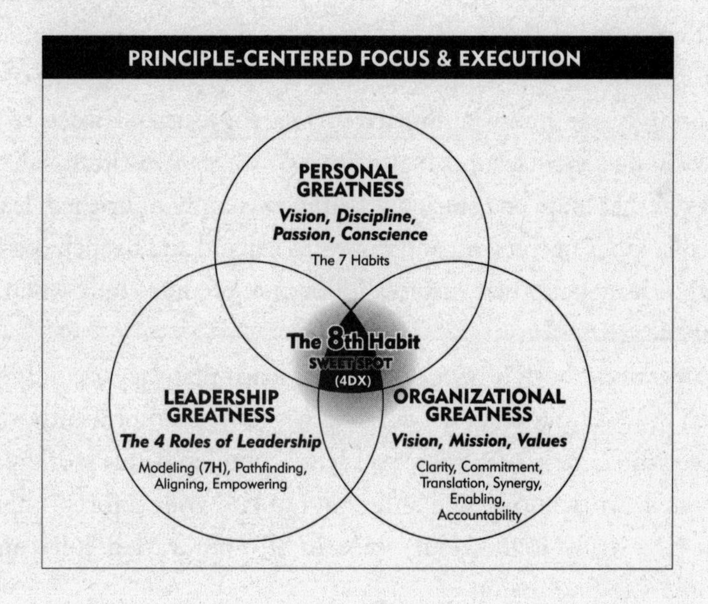

## CONCLUSION

*The 8th Habit* primarily teaches one basic paradigm: people are whole people—body, heart, mind and spirit. As we engage in the sequential 8th Habit process of finding our own voice, then making the choice to expand our influence by inspiring others to find theirs, we increase our freedom and power of choice to solve our greatest challenges and serve human needs. We learn how leadership can eventually become a choice, not a position, so that leadership is widely distributed throughout organizations and society. While we manage or control *things*, we lead (empower) *people* using the 4 Roles of Leadership: modeling, pathfinding, aligning and empowering.

We have learned that every human being is endowed with enormous potential and capacity, and the pathway to expanding that capacity is magnifying our present gifts and talents.

We have also learned that the culture we live and work in has programmed us for mediocrity, to fall short of our potential. But we have also learned that we have the power to overcome that programming, and that power inspires us to lead (empower) people, who have the power of choice.

If, through our moral authority (primary greatness) we earn formal authority or position (secondary greatness), we can institutionalize these principles so that body and spirit are being constantly nourished, leading to unbelievable kinds of freedom and power to expand and deepen our service. The kind of leadership that inspires followership comes only when we put service above self.

Organizations, both private and public, learn that they are only sustainable when they serve human needs using wisdom and moral authority.

If, over the course of a year, you have completed this workbook as it was designed, we acknowledge and congratulate your efforts. I also hope that you have truly found your voice in all your varied roles and have helped others to find theirs.

The inspiration of a noble cause involving human interests wide and far, enables men to do things they did not dream themselves capable of before, and which they were not capable of alone. The consciousness of belonging, vitally, to something beyond individuality; of being part of a personality that reaches we know not where, in space and time, greatens the heart to the limit of the soul's ideal, and builds out the supreme of character.

—*Joshua Lawrence Chamberlain*

# APPENDIX

This Appendix contains chapter-by-chapter summaries to remind you of the major ideas in each chapter.

## Chapter 1: The Pain

People face new and increasing expectations to produce more for less in a terribly complex world, yet are not allowed to use a significant portion of their talents and intelligence. Despite our gains in technology, product innovation and world markets, most people are not thriving in the organizations for which they work. They are neither fulfilled nor excited. They are frustrated. They are not clear about where the organization is headed or what its highest priorities are. They are bogged down and distracted. Most of all, they don't feel they can change much.

Voice is a unique personal significance—a significance that is revealed as you face your greatest challenges and become equal to them. Voice lies at the center of *talent* (your natural gifts and strengths), *passion* (those things that naturally excite and motivate you), *need* (including what the world needs enough to pay you for), and *conscience* (a voice within you that assures you of what is right and that prompts you to do it). When you engage in work that taps your talent and fuels your passion, therein lies your voice, your calling, your soul's code.

The best and often only way to break through pain to a lasting solution is to first understand the fundamental problem causing the pain. Much of the problem lies in behavior that flows out of an incomplete or deeply flawed paradigm or view of human nature, one that undermines people's sense of worth and straitjackets their talents and potential. Like most significant breakthroughs in human history, breaking through the pain, or creating the solution, comes from a fundamental break with old ways of thinking. If you will be patient and pay the price of understanding the root problem and then set a course of living the timeless, universal principles outlined in *The 8th Habit*, your influence will steadily grow from the inside out; you will find your voice and inspire your team and organization to find theirs in a dramatically changed world.

## Chapter 2: The Problem

The main assets and primary drivers of economic prosperity in the Industrial Age were machines and capital—*things*. People were necessary but replaceable. You could control and churn through manual workers with little consequence, as supply exceeded demand. People were like things—you could be efficient with them. When all you want is a person's body, not their mind, heart and spirit, you have reduced a person to a thing.

The problem is that managers today are still applying the Industrial Age control method to knowledge workers. Because many in positions of authority do not see the worth and potential of their people and do not possess a complete, accurate understanding of human nature, *they manage people as they do things*. This lack of understanding also prevents them from tapping into the highest motivations, talents and genius of people.

What happens when you manage people like things? They stop believing that leadership can become a choice. Most people think of leadership as a position and, therefore, don't see themselves as leaders. They think only those in positions of authority should decide what must be done. They have consented, perhaps unconsciously, to being controlled like a thing. Even if they see a need, they don't take the initiative to act. They wait to be told what to do by the person with the formal title, then respond as directed. Consequently, they blame the formal leader when things go wrong and give him or her the credit when things go well.

The widespread reluctance to take initiative or to act independently only fuels formal leaders' imperative to direct or manage their subordinates. This, they believe, is what they must do to get followers to act. And this cycle quickly escalates into codependency. Each party's weakness reinforces and ultimately justifies the other's behavior. The more a manager controls, the more he or she evokes behaviors that necessitate greater control. The codependent culture that develops eventually grows to the point at which no one takes responsibility. People disempower themselves by believing that others must change before their own circumstances can improve.

At the core, there is one simple, overarching reason why so many people remain unsatisfied in their work and why most organizations fail to draw out the greatest talent, ingenuity and creativity of their people and never become truly great, enduring organizations. It stems from an incomplete paradigm of who we are—our fundamental view of human nature.

## Chapter 3: The Solution

We've started with the *pain;* we've explored the underlying *problem;* now we will set the context for the *solution.*

Part of the solution includes learning our true nature and gifts. This helps us swim against the current and withstand negative self-interests to develop and sustain vision and determination. Knowledge of our gifts lets us take initiative and cultivate great understanding of the needs and opportunities around us. We meet the needs that match our unique talents that tap our higher motivations and that make a difference. We *find and use our voice.*

The solution has two parts: *Find Your Voice* and *Inspire Others to Find Theirs.* This is a road map for individuals at any level of an organization to maximize their fulfillment and influence, become an irreplaceable contributor and inspire their team and the broader organization to do the same.

Everyone chooses one of two roads in life. One is the broad, well-traveled road to mediocrity; the other is the road to greatness and meaning. The road to mediocrity straitjackets human potential; the path to greatness unleashes and realizes human potential. Those who choose the road to greatness become an island of excellence in a sea of mediocrity. Their example becomes contagious.

Once you've found your own voice, the choice to expand your influence and increase your contribution is the choice to inspire others to find their voice.

## Chapter 4: Discover Your Voice—Unopened Birth-Gifts

We were given magnificent *birth-gifts*—talents, capacities, privileges, intelligences, opportunities—that would remain largely unopened except through our own decision and effort. Because of these gifts, the potential within an individual is tremendous, even infinite. The more we use and magnify our present talents, the more talents we are given and the greater our capacity becomes.

Our three most important birth-gifts are:

- *Our freedom to choose*—Next to life itself, the power to choose is our greatest gift. This power and freedom stands in stark contrast to the mind-set of victimism and culture of blame so prevalent in society today. We are self-determining through our choices.
- *Natural laws or principles, which never change*—We need to live by principles rather than go along with today's culture of quick fix.
- *The four intelligences of our nature*—The four parts of our nature (body, heart, mind and spirit) correspond to four capacities, or intelligences: physical or body intelligence (PQ), emotional intelligence (EQ), mental intelligence (IQ) and spiritual intelligence (SQ).
    - Physical intelligence (PQ) includes wise nutrition; consistent, balanced exercise; proper rest, relaxation, stress management and prevention thinking.
    - Emotional intelligence (EQ) includes self-awareness, personal motivation, self-regulation, empathy and social skills.
    - Mental intelligence (IQ) includes continuous, systematic, disciplined study and education; cultivation of self-awareness; learning by teaching and doing.
    - Spiritual intelligence (SQ) includes integrity and meaning and voice.

## Chapter 5: Express Your Voice—Vision, Discipline, Passion and Conscience

Any individual who has had a profound influence on others, on institutions or on society; parents whose influence has been intergenerational; anyone who has really made a difference for good or ill possessed four common attributes: vision, discipline, passion and conscience. They represent leadership that works.

- *Vision*—The most important vision of all is to develop a sense of self, a sense of your own destiny, a sense of your unique mission and role in life, a sense of purpose and meaning.
- *Discipline*—It is the executing, the making it happen, the sacrificing to do whatever it takes to realize your vision. Discipline is willpower embodied. It is personal sacrifice, the process of subordinating today's pleasure for a greater long-term good.
- *Passion*—This comes from the heart and is manifest in optimism, excitement, emotional connection, and determination. It fires relentless drive.
- *Conscience*—It is a moral sense, an inner light and an innate sense of right and wrong. It is the voice within that is quiet, peaceful and free of ego.

## Chapter 6: Inspiring Others to Find Their Voice—The Leadership Challenge

Chapter 6 marks the beginning of Part 2: "Inspire Others to Find Their Voice" and the domain of leadership. Remember, leadership is not a formal position; it is a choice to deal with people in a way that will clearly communicate to them their worth and potential so that they will see it in themselves.

Both management and leadership are vital in an organization—either one without the other is insufficient. You can't lead things like inventories, cash flows and costs. You have to manage them. Things don't have the power and freedom to choose. Only people do. So you lead *people* and manage and control *things.*

The goal of Part 2: "Inspire Others to Find Their Voice" is to help you discover your capacity to both see and solve your problems and greatly increase your own influence and the influence of your organization—whether it be your team, department, division or entire organization, including your family.

## Chapter 7: The Voice of Influence—Be a Trim-Tab

Modeling is the spirit and center of any leadership effort. It begins with Finding Your Voice—developing the four intelligences and expressing your voice in vision, discipline, passion and conscience. Modeling is primarily done before and during the other three roles, which are pathfinding, aligning and empowering. This brings a sense of confidence and trust in the leader. But it is only after all four roles are experienced that leadership actually occurs. People then know for themselves how respected, appreciated and valued they are because others seek their opinion, respect their input, value their unique experience and genuinely involve them in the pathfinding process—they are participants.

Modeling is not just the work of an individual; it's the work of a team. When you have a team that builds on each individual's strengths and organizes to make individual weaknesses irrelevant, you have true power in an organization. So when you think of modeling, think of an individual and a complementary team.

Influence stems from your mind-set or attitude—a choice, the choice to use the voice of influence. How easy it is for people to feel, "I'm a victim; I've tried everything; there's nothing more I can do; I'm stuck." *Victimism gives our future away*. Any time we think the problem is *out there*, that very thought *is* the problem. Any time we wrap our emotional life around the weaknesses of another person, we give away our emotional freedom to that person and give him or her permission to continue to mess up our lives. Our past holds our future hostage.

Until people have found their own voice, they do not have the maturity, inner security or character strength to apply the principle-centered solution to their problem situations. Society manufactures and reinforces the mind-set of victimism and blame. But we have the power to use our birth-gifts to become the creative force of our lives and choose an approach to increase our influence.

Just as a trim-tab (the small rudder that turns the big rudder that turns the ship) influences the direction of the ship, everyone has the potential to spread their influence to determine the direction of their organization. Every organization has trim-tabbers, no matter their position. They move themselves and their team or department in such a way that they positively affect the entire organization. The trim-tab leader exercises initiative within his or her Circle of Influence.

## Chapter 8: The Voice of Trustworthiness—Modeling Character and Competence

Just as trust is the key to all relationships, so also is trust the glue that holds together organizations. Trust comes from three sources: personal, institutional and the trust that one person consciously chooses to give to another. *Trust* is both a verb and a noun. It's something shared and reciprocated between people. The fourth role (empowering) embodies making trust a verb. To develop trust, a person must be trustworthy.

Trustworthiness comes from *character and competence*. In many settings today, it is not in vogue to speak in terms of character. It's equated with soft, touchy-feely study or with someone's religion. Some wonder if our inner values matter anymore. Many believe the only things we need for success are talent, energy and personality. But history has shown that over the long term, who we *are* is more important than who we appear to be.

*Character* consists of:

- *Integrity*—You keep promises made to yourself and others.
- *Maturity*—You combine courage and compassion.
- *Abundance Mentality*—You see life as a vast array of different opportu-

nities, wealth and resources and not as a competition with only one winner.

*Competence* consists of:

- *Technical*—The skills and knowledge necessary to complete a task.
- *Conceptual*—The ability to see the big picture—to think strategically, not just tactically.
- *Interdependency*—The knowledge that the parts affect the whole—that all of life is interconnected.

Wisdom and judgment occur when character and competence intersect. More and more organizations are recognizing the need for being trustworthy, showing good character and producing trust in the culture. People are looking deeply into their own souls to sense how they, themselves, contribute to the problems and how they can contribute to the solution.

## Chapter 9: The Voice and Speed of Trust

Almost all the work of the world is done through relationships among people and in organizations. Low trust is the very definition of a bad relationship. So when organizations have low trust, the cost of doing business is high. As Stephen M. R. Covey said, "Low trust is the great hidden tax."

Relationships with high trust are easy, effortless and instantaneous. Even when mistakes are made in high-trust relationships, it hardly matters. People know you, so forget the mistake saying, "Don't worry about it; I understand." There is nothing as fast as the speed of trust. It is what holds organizations, cultures and relationships together.

Nothing destroys trust faster than making and then breaking a promise. Conversely, nothing builds and strengthens trust more than keeping a promise you make.

The Emotional Bank Account is a metaphor for the amount of trust in a relationship. The Emotional Bank Account is like a financial bank account into which you make emotional deposits and withdrawals. Deposits build trust; withdrawals erode trust. As with a financial bank account, building the Emotional Bank Accounts of others takes work and patience. Deposits require initiative, humility and sacrifice on the part of the giver. But the payoff is a high-trust relationship.

## Chapter 10: Blending Voices—Searching for the Third Alternative

The Third Alternative isn't your way—it's *our* way. It's not a compromise halfway between your way and my way; it's better than a compromise. A Third Alternative is the middle way—a higher middle position that is better than either of the other two ways, like the tip of a triangle. The Third Alternative is a better alternative than any that have been proposed. It is a product of sheer creative effort. It emerges from the overlapping vulnerabilities of two or more people—from their openness, willingness to really listen, and their desire to search.

To reach the Third Alternative, use four very important communication methods:

- Be sincerely open and listen to others to reach an understanding of what they see and why they see the world the way they do—the foundation of seeking for Third Alternatives.
- Remember that those things you experience before being presented with new information may color the way you look at that information. Communication leads to mutual understanding.
- Acknowledging that there is more than one way to interpret something. The challenge lies in creating a shared vision that accurately and honestly considers all the differing viewpoints while still remaining true to the original vision.
- Avoid communication breakdowns because of semantics—how people define words. The key thing is understanding meaning, not fighting over a symbol.

Searching for a Third Alternative requires two steps (which are not always sequential):

- Would you be willing to search for a solution that is better than what either one of you (us) has proposed?
- Would you agree to a simple ground rule: No one can make his or her point until he or she has restated the other person's point to his or her satisfaction?

## Chapter 11: One Voice—Pathfinding Shared Vision, Values and Strategy

Modeling inspires trust, and pathfinding creates order without demanding it. As soon as people agree on what matters most in an organization, they share the criteria that will drive all decisions that follow. This clarifying communication gives focus, creates order and stability and enables agility.

*Vision* on a personal scale translates into *pathfinding* in an organizational setting. Whereas individually you identify what you see to be significant, now your challenge and role is to create a shared view of what is important, of what matters most. Consider the following questions you might ask about your employees:

- Do people clearly understand organizational goals?
- Are they committed?

Helping people to clearly understand and get committed to significant goals requires you to involve them in the decision. Together you determine the organization's destination (vision and mission). Then everybody in the organization will have ownership in the path that leads to the destination (values and strategic plan).

When determining together what is most important to an organization or team, you need to understand the realities you face. Once you understand them, you work until a shared vision and values system is embodied in a mission statement and strategic plan.

Then that mission statement and strategic plan can be rolled out broadly and deeply to everyone in the organization. Co-missioning can occur where the four needs of the individual (body, mind, heart and spirit) overlap and align with the four needs of the organization (survival; growth and development; relationships; meaning, integrity and contribution). The co-missioning process is where the real power of the workforce is unleashed.

## Chapter 12: The Voice and Discipline of Execution—Aligning Goals and Systems for Results

If pathfinding identifies a path, aligning paves it. Organizations are perfectly aligned to get the results they get. Even though you may not get the results you want, the processes, structure, and systems lead to the results you are getting. Therefore, as a leader, you need to align with the results you want.

Aligning is designing and executing systems and structures that reinforce the core values and highest strategic priorities of the organization, which were selected in the pathfinding process.

Aligning involves the following actions:

- Use both personal moral authority and formal authority to create *systems* that will formalize or institutionalize your strategy and the principles embodied in your shared vision and values.
- Create *cascading goals* throughout the organization that are aligned with your shared vision, values and strategic priorities.
- Adjust and align yourselves to regular feedback you receive from the marketplace and your organization on how well you are meeting needs and delivering value.

Alignment is institutionalized trustworthiness. The very principles people have built into their value system are the basis for designing structures, systems and processes. Even if the environment, market conditions, and people change, the principles do not. The organization is the second major source of trust. When trustworthy people work within structures and systems that are not aligned with the organization's espoused values, the untrustworthy systems will dominate every time. You simply won't have trust.

## Chapter 13: The Empowering Voice—Releasing Passion and Talent

Empowering is about creating conditions that foster and release the creativity, talent, ability and potential that exists in people so they can travel the path. Unless the right conditions exist for people to make their greatest contributions, you cannot expect the best from them.

Empowering is the fruit of modeling, pathfinding and aligning—the natural result of both personal and organizational trustworthiness, which enables people to identify and unleash their human potential. It enthrones self-control, self-management and self-organization.

Successful empowerment rests in a commitment to work with team members by using a Win-Win Agreement. In an organization, win-win means the four needs of the organization (financial health, growth and development, synergistic relationships with key stakeholders and meaning/contribution) overlap with the four needs of the individual.

When empowering people and employees, leaders use a whole-person model of leadership: plan (mind), do (body), evaluate (heart) and serve (spirit). To effectively and truly empower people, you must set up the conditions of empowerment and then get out of people's way; clear their path and become a source of help as requested.

## Chapter 14: The 8th Habit and the Sweet Spot

The 8th Habit gives us a mind-set and a skill-set to constantly look for the potential in people. It is the kind of leadership that communicates to people their worth and potential so clearly that they come to see it themselves. To do this, we must listen to people. We must involve and continually affirm them by our words and through the 4 Roles of Leadership. Notice how each role directly or indirectly affirms people's worth as whole people and empowers the unleashing of their potential.

- *Modeling* (individual, team)—Inspires trust without expecting it. When people live by the principles embodied in the 8th Habit, trust (the glue of life) flourishes; trust comes only through trustworthiness. Modeling produces *moral authority*.
- *Pathfinding*—Creates order without demanding it. When people identify and are involved in strategic decisions, particularly on values and high-priority goals, they emotionally connect; the focus of both management and motivation goes from the outside to the inside. Pathfinding produces *visionary moral authority*.
- *Aligning*—Balances results and product capacity. Aligning structures, systems and processes is a form of nourishing the body politic and the spirit of trust, vision and empowerment. Aligning produces *institutionalized moral authority*.
- *Empowering*—Produces the fruit of the other three roles. It unleashes human potential without external motivation. Empowering produces cultural moral authority.

All that is covered in *The 8th Habit* can be summarized in two words: *focus* and *execution*. In these two words we truly find "simplicity on the far side of complexity." Focus deals with what matters most; execution deals with making it happen. The first two roles (modeling and pathfinding) can be summarized by the word *focus*, and the next two roles (aligning and empowering) can be summarized by the word *execution*. Focus and execution are inseparably connected. Until you have people on the same page, they will not execute consistently.

Many things effect execution, but FranklinCovey's xQ research shows that organizations have six core drivers to execution:

- *Clarity*—People clearly know what their team's or organization's goals or priorities are.

- *Commitment*—People buy in to the goals.
- *Translation*—People know what they individually need to do to help the team or organization achieve its goals.
- *Enabling*—People have the proper structure, systems or freedom to do their jobs well.
- *Synergy*—People get along or work together well.
- *Accountability*—People regularly hold each other accountable.

Breakdowns in execution typically occur as failures in one or more of these six drivers.

*The 8th Habit* explores two roads: one road leads to mediocrity, and another leads to greatness. The road to greatness contains three different kinds of greatness:

- *Personal greatness*—Found as we discover our three birth-gifts (choice, principles and the four human intelligences). When we develop these gifts and intelligences, we cultivate a magnificent character full of vision, discipline, and passion that is guided by conscience.
- *Leadership greatness*—Achieved by people who, regardless of their position, choose to inspire others to find their voice. This is achieved through living the 4 Roles of Leadership.
- *Organizational greatness*—Achieved as the organization tackles the final challenge of translating their leadership roles and work (including mission, vision and values) into the principal drivers of execution.

Organizations that govern and discipline themselves by all three kinds of greatness truly hit the *sweet spot*, which is the nexus where all three circles overlap. This nexus includes the greatest expression of power and potential, and is where the power within you is released as you find your voice as an individual, team and organization.

To close execution gaps that become roadblocks in the road to greatness, practice the 4 Disciplines of Execution. These are the solutions to the problems associated with the six core drivers to execution. These four disciplines represent 20 percent of activities that produce 80 percent of the results of executing consistently with excellence on top priorities. These 4 Disciplines are the result of the sweet spot (when the three types of greatness come together). This sweet spot is the power-releasing contact point—the set of next-step, actionable, rubber-meets-the-road, laser-focused practices that will enable a team and organization to consistently get results.

The 4 Disciplines of Execution are:

- *Discipline 1*—Focus on the wildly important.
- *Discipline 2*—Create a compelling scoreboard.
- *Discipline 3*—Translate lofty goals into specific actions.
- *Discipline 4*—Hold each other accountable all of the time.

*For more information about attending FranklinCovey's impactful workshop* 4 Disciplines of Execution, *please visit a FranklinCovey retail store or contact a FranklinCovey client partner.*

## Chapter 15: Using Our Voices Wisely to Serve Others

The inner drive to Find Your Own Voice and Inspire Others to Find Theirs is fueled by one great overarching purpose: to serve human needs. It is also the best means of achieving both. We grow more personally when we are giving ourselves to others. Our relationships improve and deepen when together we attempt to serve our family, another family, an organization, a community or some other human need.

Organizations are established to serve human needs—there is no other reason for their existence. When you successfully work with others, your own knowledge and abilities become productive, which creates a complementary team of people who possess knowledge and abilities that can compensate for and make irrelevant your own ignorance and weaknesses.

Information is not wisdom. Information and knowledge coupled with worthy purposes and principles is wisdom. It is the child of integrity—being integrated around principles. And integrity is the child of humility and courage. Wisdom comes to people who educate and obey their conscience.

Wisdom teaches us to respect all people, to celebrate their differences, to be guided by a single ethic—service above self. Power and moral supremacy emerge from humility, where the greatest becomes the servant of all. Moral authority is achieved through sacrifice. Robert K. Greenleaf wrote, ". . . [T]he only authority deserving one's allegiance is that which is freely and knowingly granted by the led to the leader in response to, and in proportion to, the clearly evident servant stature of the leader." The very top people of truly great organizations are servant-leaders because they are the most humble, reverent, open, teachable, respectful and caring. Servant-leaders build enduring greatness in their organizations.

When people use their formal authority early on, their moral authority lessens. When you borrow strength from position, you build weakness in three places: self (because you are not developing moral authority), others (because they become co-dependent with your use of formal authority) and relationship quality (because the authentic openness and trust never develops).

You can make Find Your Voice and Inspire Others to Find Theirs a deeply ingrained habit of knowledge, attitude and skill. Just listen to your own conscience and source of wisdom.

## Journal

Record notes, thoughts or impressions from Chapter 1.

Record notes, thoughts or impressions from Chapter 2.

Record notes, thoughts or impressions from Chapter 3.

Record notes, thoughts or impressions from Chapter 4.

Record notes, thoughts or impressions from Chapter 5.

Record notes, thoughts or impressions from Chapter 6.

Record notes, thoughts or impressions from Chapter 7.

Record notes, thoughts or impressions from Chapter 8.

Record notes, thoughts or impressions from Chapter 9.

Record notes, thoughts or impressions from Chapter 10.

Record notes, thoughts or impressions from Chapter 11.

Record notes, thoughts or impressions from Chapter 12.

Record notes, thoughts or impressions from Chapter 13.

Record notes, thoughts or impressions from Chapter 14.

Record notes, thoughts or impressions from Chapter 15.

# ACKNOWLEDGMENTS

So many talented people have contributed to, improved and helped launch this *Personal Workbook*. To each I express my deep gratitude and appreciation:

- To my many FranklinCovey colleagues, particularly Lisa Daems and Nancy Greenwood, and Annie Oswald, Debra Lund, Jennifer Tate, Deborah Burkett, Bill Bennett and Bob Whitman, and my sons Sean Covey and David Covey. Special thanks to the Stephen R. Covey Group team—Darla Salin, Julie Gillman, Julie Hillyard, Sonia Larson, Kara Holmes and Chelsea Johns—for their constant enabling and synergistic support. Finally, to Boyd Craig, my partner in this project, for his championing leadership, judgment and content expertise that made *The 8th Habit* and this *Personal Workbook* a reality.
- To my "dynamic duo" agents, Jan Miller and Shannon Miser-Marven, and the entire Dupree/Miller & Associates team.
- To my publishing associates at Simon & Schuster: Wylie O'Sullivan, Michele Jacob, Courtney Morrow, Carisa Hays, Phil Metcalf, Erich Hobbing, Dominick Anfuso, Martha Levin and Carolyn Reidy.
- To FranklinCovey's many clients and other organizations and leaders the world over who are models of 8th Habit leadership.
- And finally, to my wife, Sandra, our nine children and their spouses, our forty-seven grandchildren, my brother and sisters, and my parents, grandparents and ancestors—who, with our eternal Father and God, have shaped and blessed my life beyond measure.

# ABOUT THE AUTHOR

Stephen R. Covey is an internationally respected leadership authority, family expert, teacher, organizational consultant and author who has dedicated his life to teaching principle-centered living and leadership to build both families and organizations. He holds an M.B.A. from Harvard and a doctorate from Brigham Young University, where he was a professor of organizational behavior and business management.

Dr. Covey is the author of several acclaimed books, including the international bestseller *The 7 Habits of Highly Effective People*, which was named the #1 Most Influential Business Book of the Twentieth Century and one of the top-ten most influential management books ever. It has sold more than fifteen million copies in thirty-eight languages throughout the world. Other bestsellers include *The 8th Habit: From Effectiveness to Greatness; First Things First*, *Principle-Centered Leadership; The 7 Habits of Highly Effective Families; The Nature of Leadership* and *Living the 7 Habits*, bringing the combined total to over 20 million books sold.

As the father of nine and grandfather of forty-three, he received the 2003 Fatherhood Award from the National Fatherhood Initiative, which he says is the most meaningful award he has ever received. Other awards given to Dr. Covey include the Thomas More College Medallion for continuing service to humanity, the National Speakers Association Speaker of the Year in 1999, the Toastmasters Golden Gavel award in 2004, the Sikh's 1998 International Man of Peace award, the 1994 International Entrepreneur of the Year award and the National Entrepreneur of the Year Lifetime Achievement award for Entrepreneurial Leadership. Dr. Covey has also been recognized as one of *Time* magazine's 25 Most Influential Americans and has received seven honorary doctorate degrees.

Dr. Covey is the co-founder and vice chairman of FranklinCovey Company, the leading global professional services firm with thirty-seven international offices serving more than 100 countries. They share Dr. Covey's vision, discipline and passion to enable greatness in people and organizations everywhere.

www.StephenCovey.com

# ABOUT FRANKLINCOVEY

## MISSION STATEMENT

*We enable greatness in people and organizations everywhere.*

## FOUNDATIONAL BELIEFS

*We believe—*

1. People are inherently capable, aspire to greatness and have the power to choose.
2. Principles are timeless and universal, and are the foundation for lasting effectiveness.
3. Leadership is a choice, built inside out on a foundation of character. Great leaders unleash the collective talent and passion of people toward the right goal.
4. Habits of effectiveness come only from the committed use of integrated processes and tools.
5. Sustained superior performance requires P/PC Balance®—a focus on achieving results *and* on building capability.

## VALUES

1. Commitment to Principles. We are passionate about our content, and strive to be models of the principles and practices we teach.
2. Lasting Customer Impact. We are relentless about delivering on our promises to our customers. Our success comes only with their success.
3. Respect for the Whole Person. We value each other and treat each person with whom we work as true partners.
4. Profitable Growth. We embrace profitability and growth as the life-blood of our organization; they give us the freedom to fulfill our mission and vision.

FranklinCovey (NYSE:FC) is the global leader in effectiveness training, productivity tools and assessment services for organizations and individuals.

FranklinCovey helps organizations succeed by unleashing the power of their workforce to focus on and execute their top priorities. Clients include 90 percent of the Fortune 100, more than 75 percent of the Fortune 500, thousands of small and midsized businesses, as well as numerous government entities and educational institutions. Organizations and individuals access FranklinCovey products and services through corporate training, licensed client facilitators, one-on-one coaching, public workshops, catalogs, more than 100 retail stores and *www.franklincovey.com*. FranklinCovey has nearly 1500 associates providing professional services and products in the United States and for thirty-seven international offices, serving more than 100 countries.

## PROGRAMS AND SERVICES

- xQ Survey and Debrief *(to help leaders assess their organization's "Execution Quotient")*
- The 7 Habits of Highly Effective People workshop
- The 7 Habits for Managers
- The 4 Disciplines of Execution for Business Results Consulting Services
- FOCUS: Achieving Your Highest Priorities workshop
- The 4 Roles of Leadership workshop
- The FranklinCovey Planning System
- Writing Advantage Workshop
- Project Management
- Business Acumen Workshop

To learn more about FranklinCovey products and services, please call 1-888-868-1776 or 1-801-817-1776, or go to www.franklincovey.com.